Materialism, Minds, and Cartesian Dualism

Materialism, Minds, and Cartesian Dualism

Robert Francis Almeder

HAMILTON BOOKS
AN IMPRINT OF
ROWMAN & LITTLEFIELD
Lanham • Boulder • New York • London

Published by Hamilton Books
An imprint of The Rowman & Littlefield Publishing Group, Inc.
4501 Forbes Boulevard, Suite 200, Lanham, Maryland 20706
www.rowman.com

86-90 Paul Street, London EC2A 4NE, United Kingdom

Copyright © 2022 by The Rowman & Littlefield Publishing Group, Inc.

All rights reserved. No part of this book may be reproduced in any form or by any electronic or mechanical means, including information storage and retrieval systems, without written permission from the publisher, except by a reviewer who may quote passages in a review.

British Library Cataloguing in Publication Information Available

Library of Congress Cataloging-in-Publication Data Available
Names: Almeder, Robert F., author.
Title: Materialism, minds, and Cartesian dualism / Robert Francis Almeder.
Description: Lanham : Hamilton Books, an imprint of Rowman & Littlefield, [2022] | Includes bibliographical references. | Summary: "The book takes well-established, scientific evidence on consciousness to interrogate, and re envisions questions of personal reincarnation and thus of the mind/body problem. Methodologically, the basis of the book is rooted in the careful argumentation and logical appraisal of classical materialism and the history of the mind-body problem"—Provided by publisher.
Identifiers: LCCN 2021048984 (print) | LCCN 2021048985 (ebook) | ISBN 9780761872931 (paperback) | ISBN 9780761872948 (epub)
Subjects: LCSH: Philosophical anthropology. | Mind and body. | Materialism. | Reincarnation.
Classification: LCC BD450 .A4729 2022 (print) | LCC BD450 (ebook) | DDC 128—dc23/eng/20211202
LC record available at https://lccn.loc.gov/2021048984
LC ebook record available at https://lccn.loc.gov/2021048985

*For Ginny, Lisa, and Melanie,
my nearest and dearest,
whose love and support
has sustained me.*

Contents

Acknowledgments	ix
Foreword	xi
Introduction	1
Chapter 1: Basic Objections to Mind-Body Dualism Advanced by Reductive Materialists	3
Chapter 2: Evidence Favoring Cartesian Mind-Body Dualism and Reincarnation	21
Chapter 3: Objections and Replies to the Minimalist View of Personal Reincarnation	67
Chapter 4: Where Are We Now?	89
Appendix: A. J. Ayer on Personal Reincarnation	97
References	101
Additional Suggested Reading	105
Index	109
About the Author	115

Acknowledgments

There are uncountably many people, universities, and institutions, who have helped me with this work culminating a lifetime of serious scholarship. I have been able to thank many of them in earlier publications, including Ian Stevenson, who inspired me to write a series of works on Mind and Body. Nicholas Rescher, above all others, has been an inspiration and an invaluable colleague over the years. The Pittsburgh Center for the History and Philosophy of Science provided me with the time and collegiality for my research. Chapter 4 and the "Suggested Reading" list at the end of this book note some of the many scholars and researchers to whom I owe a debt of gratitude for their inspiration and assistance.

Among others, Jonathan Sisk and Rowman and Littlefield supported my earlier work on reincarnation. I would also like to thank The Fulbright Foundation for their generous funding of the project's early drafting and for providing for my stay, lectures, and scholarship at the Federal University of Juiz de Fora (UFJF), Brazil. The School of Medicine at UFJF, Brazil was a dynamic and very supportive community. In particular, I would like to thank the generous Alexander Moreira-Almeida and his colleagues. Franklin Santana Santos, included an earlier essay on this material in *Exploring Frontiers of the Mind-Body Relationship* (Springer Press, 2011).

Thank you to Rebecca Kinney who provided invaluable assistance in the preparation of the manuscript. Thank you to Sam Brawand, copyeditor extraordinaire, for her discerning mind and eye. And a special thanks to my daughter, Melanie, whose support insured that this book could be completed.

Foreword

This book is about humans and whether humans are basically a collection of atoms that simply happened and evolved slowly on earth over billions of years under the laws of physics and natural selection.

Some people, of course, think that humans must have emerged originally from a clashing random collection of uncountabe atoms ultimately forming physical objects from which we sprung, somehow under natural selection and the laws of physics. They also think our whole world is made up of only physical (material) objects, and that the atoms unpredictably came to establish our world so very long ago.

Other people, however, think there is more to it than that. Much more indeed. They think rather that there are some immaterial or unobservable substances lurking about somewhere in or near our bodies or brains, and that they combine sometimes or interact with our bodies (material substance) to produce or to cause actions that mysteriously allow us to evolve further under natural selection. For these people, humans are accordingly comprised of two distinctly different kinds of substances: material substances and immaterial substances. They believe that these different substances often interact with each other in order to produce or to cause human behaviors.

So, what is the problem? Well, some people insist that we are just bodies with brains, both of which are material substances. For these people (call them materialists), we are physical machines; nothing but material substances in this glorious world governed by the laws of physics. No ghosts, angels, or gods in the machine. No spiritual substances (like a "soul") or an immaterial substance anywhere. We are here today; gone tomorrow, dust-to-dust whether we like it or not.

So the "Mind-Body Problem" is that other people disagree with materialists because they, unlike materialists, believe in mental events (or immaterial substances) such as being conscious, loving, hating, wishing, wanting, hoping, believing, knowing, intending, feeling tired, or feeling pain, and which they imagine are mental states but are not physical states or material substances.

In short, the problem as it now exists is simply a matter of successfully determining who has the right answer on whether the materialist is correct, or whether the non-materialist is correct. Non-materialists believe that humans are distinct composites of both material and immaterial substances that causally interact.

Some philosophers and scientists argue, as you will see in pages of this book, that there is no scientific way to solve this problem, and thus by implication determine how mysterious we are. With these latter skeptics I firmly disagree for several reasons, and that is why I wrote this book.

Still others believe that the mind-body problem allows for belief in both kinds of substance (material and immaterial); but that the real problem here is how these two distinctly different kinds of substance possibly interact causally one on or with the other. After all, for this group these two distinct kinds of substance seem to have nothing in common that would allow for a causal interaction of any sort.

At any rate, in the following pages you will also encounter an important empirical argument that some humans have in fact personally reincarnated. As incredible as that may sound, this general argument roots solely in strong empirical data, and not on any superstitious, religious, or philosophical considerations. We do not know why or what causal mechanisms are involved. I call it a minimalist theory of reincarnation. Chapter 2 of this book defends more fully the philosophical and empirical consequences of this argument.

In an earlier book, *Death and Personal Survival: The Evidence for Life After Death* (1992), I explored a somewhat less compelling, general form of the argument for personal reincarnation inspired earlier by Ian Stevenson and his colleagues, an argument to which I was then and remain irresistibly drawn. I hope that most readers will read this revision on what is at least a strong argument based on strong empirical evidence.

Because that earlier book elicited a fair measure of criticism, I sought in subsequent publications to reply to and expand the main argument to include more data and reflection on the issue in an effort to update Stevenson's research, and thereby render more persuasive the general argument and its broader contours not treated in the earlier book.

Incidentally, in that earlier book I had also urged, among other items, that it would be irrational for us not to accept the belief based on the argument offered that some people have reincarnated. Several people think that this latter claim is a bit over the top, so to speak. However, I responded elsewhere to that criticism, including sections in the chapters 2 and 3 of this book.

Finally, the critical case studies examined over the years by Ian Stevenson and his research colleagues at the University of Virginia, and their acute

responses to hasty critics, is a paradigm example of a breakthrough on the scientific status of the belief that some people have reincarnated.
Robert Almeder, PhD
Distinguished Professor Emeritus of Philosophy
Georgia State University
Atlanta, Georgia.

Introduction

The view that natural science has refuted the belief that human beings are made up of two distinct kinds of substances, namely, Cartesian Material Substances (bodies) and Cartesian Immaterial Substances (souls or minds) that causally interact with each other, is pervasive. This view affirms robustly that only physical objects exist in this world governed by the laws of physics. So there cannot be immaterial minds (or souls or Cartesian Egos) in addition to physical bodies and brains when we seek to explain human behavior by appeal to such mental events as belief, desire, intention, knowing, pain, joy, loving, and hating, conceived as non-physical causes of behavior. Call this "reductive materialism."

Indeed, for well over the twentieth century, and stretching back even as far as the ancient atomists, some form of reductive materialism has ruled the roost, crowing that if minds or mental events are not ultimately reducible to, or identical with, some set of brain states, or some complex computational function of brains, or some biological property produced by the brain, then there are no minds or mental events.

Nevertheless, there are critics who reject reductive materialism. They accept belief in non-physical minds as affirmed by Plato, Aristotle, the Medievals, Descartes, and so many other Cartesian dualists. Indeed, many philosophers and scientists believe that mental events are not physical events. Predictably, reductive materialists respond to them that belief in Cartesian immaterial substances is just too unjustifiable for any serious thinker to accept.

Doubtless, we still hear voices crying out in the wilderness that reductive materialism may not be true, or even that it is demonstrably false (see, for example, Broad 1925; Chalmers 1996; Levine 2001; review of Levine 2001, by Horgan 2006; Swinburne 1984; Kim 2005). But it often seems that the vast majority of scientists and philosophers continue to regard those voices as the unfortunate legacy of tenaciously entrenched superstition, rank stupidity, or religion. For that majority, whatever else the mind-body problem may be, it will not talk to the question of whether there are Cartesian immaterial substances that cause certain human behaviors and are somehow irreducible to any physical property, complex or otherwise, chemical or biological, of the brain.

So, what are the materialist objections to belief in the denial of reductive materialism, and what are the basic reasons reductive materialists advance in favor of reductive materialism? And, what is the evidence that favors mind-body Cartesian dualism? What can we say about these questions that have not been said?

In examining the basic objections to mind-body dualism advanced by reductive materialists, I shall urge in chapter 1 that those objections are demonstrably bankrupt. Thereafter, in chapter 2, I will argue that there is a compelling empirical and currently available body of evidence favoring Cartesian mind-body dualism. The available evidence in question is based, in part, upon the acceptance of what I will describe and defend as a minimalist theory of personal reincarnation. As theories go, it has deductive implications at the sensory level, and, as we shall see, has been well confirmed empirically.

There are several other kinds of empirical evidence favoring Cartesian mind-body dualism, and personal survival of some sort. However, I leave that body of evidence and discussion for others to re-examine elsewhere.

The conclusion offered in these following pages is modest in asserting the belief that the reductionist posture of contemporary materialism against the existence of Cartesian immaterial substances appears more dogmatic than anything else. Accordingly, the promise of reductive materialism in describing and explaining human behaviors seems unlikely to emerge any time soon, if ever.

Chapter 1

Basic Objections to Mind-Body Dualism Advanced by Reductive Materialists

FIVE OBJECTIONS TO CARTESIAN IMMATERIAL SUBSTANCES

The first, and probably the most popular objection we hear from reductive materialists is that the belief in the existence of Cartesian immaterial substances is not empirically testable or verifiable; and so it must fall squarely into the domain of philosophy, or religion, or simply arises and exists from ignorance or superstition.

If we then ask what is wrong with this issue turning out to be a philosophical matter, the typical answer will likely be that philosophers, unlike reputable scientists, have never really been able to agree on anything non-trivial. René Descartes (1985) was right, they say, in noting this *scandalum philosophiae* (all other things being equal; scandal in philosophy), but, so this objection goes, in spite of his deepest aspiration to the contrary, Descartes was never quite able to overcome that scandal by advancing his well-known attempt to place philosophy on a firm methodological footing that would allow for something much like the *certainty we find in mathematical knowledge about our world.*

By way of contrast, at least all serious scientists will, by their methods, agree that there are certain nomic regularities (causal physical laws) allowing us to predict, *ceteris paribus*, precisely our sensory experience and certain physical events allowing for our greater adaptability under natural selection.

However enduring this first verificationist objection to Cartesian mind-body dualism may be, it arguably underestimates how much philosophers have agreed upon and overestimates how much scientists have agreed upon, even in the face of theories allowing for very reliable predictions.

While we cannot here pursue it at length, most philosophers have generally agreed, for example, that if we take classical logic seriously, philosophical solipsism (that is, the thesis that I am the only human) is indefensible, and most agree that it has been irreversibly refuted, although certainly not in any laboratory setting or in any experimental or non-experimental test.

That refutation, incidentally, occurred first when Christine Ladd Franklin wrote to Bertrand Russell and asserted that she had found Russell's defense of personal solipsism compelling and that, as a result, she too was a solipsist. It appears that Russell thought she was serious, and that she had not intended to offer a decisive counterexample to any argument favoring Russell's thesis. If both of them were solipsists, of course, Russell's argument would be logically incoherent, or self-defeating whatever reasons anybody offered for it. Did Russell really believe that Franklin was an illusion that sent him a counter example? (see Almeder 1998; Russell 2009).

On the one hand, Philosophers also generally agreed that Aristotle's view that non-human animals are not rational because they do not think (because they allegedly showed no capacity to relate means to ends or to use tools) stands refuted or falsified certainly by Jane Goodall's pioneering research on chimps and gorillas. Aristotle's philosophical thesis was empirically falsified, and all philosophers pretty much agree on that.

On the other hand, however well confirmed a scientific thesis may be, that in itself does not show it to be objectively true. The history of natural science is replete with claims that were once well-confirmed and enthusiastically accepted as true by the scientific community at large only to find at a later date that those same theses were no longer as acceptable or confirmed in the light of new evidence. Ptolemaic Astronomy, Absolute Space and Time, the Caloric Theory of Heat, and the Phlogiston Theory of Combustion come readily to mind as suitable examples of such occurrences.

The second objection we often find in the natural sciences is that, contrary to the main point just offered, belief in Cartesian immaterial substance is indeed empirically testable, that it has been tested but not confirmed. And so, we have no confirming or verifying empirical evidence for it.

The third objection we will see below is that the belief in Cartesian Immaterial substance is indeed empirically testable, but science shows that souls, or Cartesian immaterial substances, cannot exist because contemporary science shows that consciousness, or any mental state whatever, at least as traditionally conceived, cannot exist after human brain death.

The fourth objection to Cartesian dualism is that we simply do not need Cartesian immaterial substances in order to explain anything at all; and the fifth objection against Cartesian immaterial substances, moreover, could not in principle serve as causes for anything in this world, and so their existence would explain nothing that transpires in this world. Consequently, they could have no explanatory power sufficient to explain human behavior or anything else.

In the remaining pages of this chapter, I will examine closely these last four objections to Cartesian mind-body dualism and urge that these four core objections are insufficiently persuasive. But not because the Cartesian thesis is not testable. It is empirically testable, and in different ways.

Thereafter, in chapter 2, I will assert an argument that while there is no empirical or scientific evidence that Cartesian immaterial substances *do not* exist, there is plenty of robust empirical evidence that they *do* exist.

Summing up, this chapter will show why the core objections to belief in Cartesian immaterial substances fail. Chapter 2 will examine strong empirical evidence favoring belief in the existence of Cartesian immaterial substances, and that natural science therefore can confirm the existence of causal agents in the world-causal agents that science may not be able to discuss easily as long as the concept of a cause is understood solely in terms of the properties of physical objects, as we ordinarily understand them.

We turn now to chapter 1 and to Derek Parfit's (1984) argument that belief in Cartesian immaterial substances is certainly an empirically testable thesis, but that we never got the evidence needed that would confirm it. Then we will scrutinize John R. Searle's (1992) claim that science has shown that Cartesian immaterial substances cannot exist. And after that, we will see the objection that there is no need to believe in Cartesian immaterial substances, and then that appeal to such entities could explain nothing because they could not serve as causes of anything.

ANTI-REDUCTIONISM IS IN PRINCIPLE CONFIRMABLE, BUT UNCONFIRMED

Parfit's Argument Examined

In Parfit's (1984) delightful and rigorous book *Reasons and Persons*, under a heading number "82" titled "How a Non-Reductionist View Might Have Been True," he wrote:

> Some writers claim that the concept of a Cartesian Ego is unintelligible. I doubt this claim. And I believe that there might have been evidence supporting the Cartesian View.
>
> There might, for example, have been evidence supporting the belief in reincarnation. One such piece of evidence might be this. A Japanese woman might claim to remember living a life as a Celtic hunter and warrior in the Bronze Age. On the basis of her apparent memories she might make many predictions that could be checked by archaeologists. Thus, she might claim to remember having a bronze bracelet, shaped like two fighting dragons. And she might claim that

she remembers burying this bracelet beside some particular megalith, just before the battle in which she was killed. Archaeologists might now find just such a bracelet buried in this spot, and their instruments might show that the earth had not been disturbed for at least 2,000 years. This Japanese woman might make many other such predictions, all of which are verified.

Suppose next that there are countless other cases in which people alive today claim to remember living certain past lives and provide similar predictions that are all verified. This becomes true of most of the people in the world's population. If there was enough such evidence, and there was no other way in which we could explain how most of us could know such detailed facts about the distant past, we might have to concede that we have accurate quasi-memories about past lives. We might have to conclude that the Japanese woman has a way of knowing about the life of a Celtic Bronze Age warrior which is like her memory of her own life.

It might next be discovered that there is no physical continuity between the Celtic warrior and the Japanese woman. We might therefore have to abandon the belief that the carrier of memory is the brain. We might have to assume that the cause of these quasi-memories is something purely mental. We might have to assume that there is some purely mental entity, which was in some way involved in the life of the Celtic warrior, and is now in some way involved in the life of the Japanese woman, and which has continued to exist during the thousands of years that have separated the lives of these two people. A Cartesian Ego is just such an entity. If there was sufficient evidence of reincarnation, we might have reason to believe that there really are such entities. And we might then reasonably conclude that such an entity is what each of us really is.

This kind of evidence would not directly support the claim that Cartesian Egos have other special properties in which Cartesians believe. It would not show that the continued existence of these Egos is all-or-nothing. But there might have been evidence to support this claim. There might have been various kinds or degrees of damage to a person's brain which did not in any fundamental way alter this person, while other kinds or degrees of damage seemed to produce a completely new person, in no way psychologically continuous with the original person. Something similar might have been true of the various kinds of mental illness. We might have generally reached the conclusion that these kinds of interference either did nothing at all to destroy psychological continuity, or destroyed it completely. It might have proved impossible to find, or to produce, immediate cases, in which psychological connectedness held to reduced degrees.

Have we good evidence for the belief in reincarnation? And have we evidence to believe that psychological continuity depends chiefly not on the continuity of the brain but on the continuity of some other entity, which either exists unimpaired, or does not exist at all? We do not in fact have the kind of evidence described above. Even if we can understand the concept of a Cartesian Pure Ego, or spiritual substance, we do not have evidence to believe such entities

> exist. Nor do we have evidence to believe that a person is any other kind of separately existing entity. And we have much evidence both to believe that the carrier of psychological continuity is the brain, and to believe that psychological connectedness could hold to any reduced degree.
>
> I have conceded that the best-known version of the Non-Reductionist View, which claims that we are Cartesian Egos, may make sense. And I have suggested that, if the facts had been very different, there might have been sufficient evidence to justify belief in this view. (Parfit 1984, 227–29)

Parfit's (1984) argument avoids a facile dogmatism that comes of casually affirming that belief in the existence of Cartesian immaterial substance is obviously unintelligible. From a certain point of view such an assertion might be unintelligible, but whether that point of view is in fact defensible, or possibly adopted as philosophical dogma, would still be an open question. Rather than take the dogmatic stance, Parfit seems instead to reply to the question "What should we take as robustly solid evidence that Cartesian immaterial substances exist?"

Along with A. J. Ayer (1956) in *The Problem of Knowledge*, Parfit (1971a; 1984; 2001) affirms that the thesis is in fact empirically testable under a minimalist construal of personal reincarnation because, he says, the reincarnation hypothesis makes predictions or has test implications, as long as we accept as a necessary condition for personal identity that one have systemic personal memories that nobody else could have.

After all, if the person sitting beside you professed to be Julius Caesar in a new body and to having personal memories that only Julius Caesar could have had, and indeed had a number of such memories, and if we could find no other equally plausible way to explain how he got the memories of Julius Caesar, then, assuming also that we had a large number of similar cases, we would be faced with the conclusion that we have sterling evidence here that the person beside you is, in fact, Julius Caesar. Indeed, if he really is Julius Caesar in a different body, then he should have empirically verifiable and confirmable personal memories that only Julius Caesar could have had.

He might, for example, tell you that he had a twin brother, Caius, who for certain reasons never left the family farm, and that he, Julius Caesar, had buried at a specific location beside the Rubicon River, just before crossing it in 49 BC, a sum of 400 newly minted gold coins and a personal note leaving the money to Caius, just in case he was killed in Rome the following week. He also tells you that he had instructed one of his soldiers, Cratylus, to go to his family secretly and inform them of the whereabouts of the buried gold coins for Caius. Such memory claims would indeed be empirically confirmable in the way suggested by Parfit. Certainly, too, there is no current record anywhere that Caesar had an identical twin brother, or that he, Caesar, indeed buried that sum of money with a note leaving the money to his twin brother Caius. Assuming, then, that we go to the place where the money is supposedly buried, excavate the ground, assured by famous paleontologists that the ground has not been disturbed at that site since 49 BC, and find the minted gold coins and the note (authenticated by expert graphologists) in the handwriting of Julius Caesar.

Suppose further that the person beside you continues and tells you many other similar memories he has, and suppose they are all confirmed in much the same way. How would we explain his having these confirmed memories that only Julius Caesar could have had? What would be the best available and non-arbitrary explanation for this person having these confirmed personal memories if it is not that this person beside you is indeed Julius Caesar in a new body?

Certainly most people would take such evidence as confirming that this person is Julius Caesar in a new body and sitting beside you. That is because most people instinctively believe in the memory theory of personal identity, which neither Parfit nor Ayer questioned.

If we could not come up with an alternative empirically testable hypothesis that would produce the same effects without our having to believe that the person beside you is Julius Caesar in a new body, and if there were many other cases like this, then we would have little choice but to accept that, at least, this person beside you is reincarnated, by some causal mechanism we know not what, and for some reason we know not why.

DEFENDING THE MEMORY THEORY OF IDENTITY

On this last point, incidentally, and as a brief defense of the memory theory of personal identity, the major objection to any memory theory of personal identity was offered early by Thomas Reid (1785) *Essays on the Intellectual Powers of Man* (essay 3, chap. 6; cited in Williams 1956–1957, 229–53).

The major objection consists in a thought experiment in which a fellow named Charles turns up claiming to be Guy Fawkes, a famous British criminal. All Charles' memory claims can be checked to fit the life of Fawkes, and those facts that cannot be directly verified, will at least be plausible, and provide explanation of unexplained facts. And so under the memory theory of personal identity, Charles is Guy Fawkes in a new body.

Williams (1956–1957) asks us now to imagine another person, Robert, who turns up and satisfies the memory criteria for being Guy Fawkes equally well. We cannot say that both of them are identical with Fawkes, which they are not because they live different lives, and have different thoughts and feelings for each other because if they were both indeed Fawkes then they would be identical to each other. So, Williams concludes that apparent systematic memories cannot constitute personal identity. This basic objection has managed to convince the majority of writers that something more like bodily continuity than memory would account for personal identity.

One might respond, however, that this counterexample is invalid because if Robert were to show up after Charles, while satisfying the memory criteria for being Fawkes, that would be an empirical disproof, or falsification, of memory criteria for personal identity.

The attractiveness of the memory criteria for personal identity is that it is in fact empirically falsifiable just in case somebody other than Charles was to show up with the same memories of Fawkes.

The fact that we can imagine the empirical conditions that would falsify the memory theory, is not a logical refutation of the theory. Rather, it is a statement of conditions that would be sufficient to empirically refute the theory.

Presumably, we would, or at least we should, agree that if Robert had the same personal memories as Fawkes, while Charles has them also, the memory theory of personal identity would stand refuted. But of course that has not happened just yet, and so the memory theory cannot simply be dismissed by appeal to what we would accept as empirical evidence for the falsity of the memory theory of personal identity.

I know of no other persuasive counterexample to the memory theory of personal identity. In fact, given that the thesis is empirically falsifiable, it seems logically bizarre to offer any counterexample about what might happen if something were to occur and then claim that, as a result, the theory has in fact been empirically refuted.

Along with Parfit (1971a; 1984; 2001) and Ayer (1956), and assuming we retain systemically unique memories as at least a necessary condition for personal identity, and if something like the above example came to pass often enough, we would need to change dramatically what we mean by "memory."

After all, as Parfit (1971a; 1971b; 1984; 2001) and others remind us, we cannot gainfully define "memory" in terms of some biological product of the brain, or some neural network, or any describable biochemical property or complex set of neurobiological properties, ultimately defined in terms of atoms and molecules that are governed by the laws of physics at some fundamental level and that cease to exist with the death of the brain. Those things die with brain death.

But if this person beside you has the confirmed personal memories of Julius Caesar, and if Julius Caesar's memories were identifiable with the above stated properties or biological properties produced by the brain, clearly this person could not have the memories they do have. So, belief in the existence of Cartesian Immaterial Substance is an empirically confirmable hypothesis.

We can only wonder why so little has been said about this, given the general assumption so widely adopted that whether anything like a Cartesian Mind exists is a question of metaphysics (in the pejorative sense) and not something that is empirically confirmable or testable in natural science.

So, as Parfit (1984) again adds, while belief in personal reincarnation and, by implication, in Cartesian Immaterial Substance, is certainly an empirically testable and confirmable hypothesis, we do not in fact have any such evidence for believing in reincarnation.

The above-cited Parfit (1984) text asserts that the thesis has been tested, but that we never got the confirming evidence to warrant acceptance of Cartesian immaterial substances, and so we have no rational justification now for accepting the thesis (227–29).

This conclusion emerges because Parfit, unlike Ayer, thinks a necessary condition for accepting the thesis would require most of the current population to have such confirmed memories before we could say of anyone in particular that they are a reincarnated person.

That requirement seems an unnecessarily strong requirement, rather than say a requirement to the effect that there be, over time, a large number of such cases, sufficient to establish the non-anecdotal nature of the evidence offered.

If that is so, then Parfit's position would be that science has at least indirectly refuted the Cartesian position by indirectly refuting the thesis of personal reincarnation, which he apparently takes to be the best available hypothesis under which Cartesian mind-body dualism is at least empirically testable. Apart from that, he offers us no explicit help in what it would take to disconfirm either personal reincarnation or mind-body dualism under some other hypothesis.

AYER'S ARGUMENT EXAMINED

Nor should we forget, incidentally, that Ayer's (1956) in his *Problem of Knowledge*, in the course of arguing for memory as the criterion for personal identity, argues that if the man sitting beside you had the memories of Caesar Augustus, better yet had memories that only Caesar Augustus could have had, and such memories were independently confirmed, then we would need to say that the man beside you is indeed Caesar Augustus in a different body, unless we could find some way to confirm the belief that one could have the memories that only Caesar Augustus could have without being Caesar Augustus. Ayer, like Parfit, had no hesitation in accepting the view that the existence of minds is an empirical hypothesis testable under the hypothesis of reincarnation.

In fact, however, Ayer did not believe ostensibly in personal reincarnation, but used it rather as a thought experiment to drive home what we would say if the evidence for reincarnation were actually obtained. Clearly he took the existence of Cartesian minds, by implication, to be an empirically testable thesis as long as one accepts the memory theory of personal identity. This conclusion was orthogonal to his well-published view that empirical hypotheses that are central to the sciences are not at the core of philosophy (Ayer 1994, 1–17; Ayer 1956, 187–200). One would have expected that the mind-body problem be at the core of philosophy, but his granting it empirical status as a testable empirical hypothesis would place it squarely inside natural science.

In the end, what seems objectionable in Parfit's (1984) claim that we do not have the required evidence for justified belief in reincarnation is simply that he lays down an impossibly strong requirement, namely that most of the current population have at the same time empirically confirmed past life memories that only the former person could have had.

Fortunately, Ayer made no such demand rather than that there simply are many other past similar cases of confirmed memories. More on Ayer's view later (see appendix).

Now turn briefly to Searle's (1992) position which he offered as evidence for the claim that science has shown that traditional or Cartesian mind-body dualism is false, and not simply that we do not have enough evidence for it.

ANTI-REDUCTIONISM IS FALSE?

Searle's Argument

In *The Rediscovery of Mind*, after asserting that all mental events are biological phenomena, John Searle (1992) goes on to offer a general defense of his position. He says:

> They are as much the result of biological evolution as any other phenotype. Consciousness, in short, is a biological feature of human and certain animal brains. It is caused by neurobiological processes and is as much a part of the natural biological order as any other biological features such as photosynthesis, digestion, or mitosis. This principle is the first stage in understanding the place of consciousness within our worldview. The thesis of this chapter so far has been that once you see that atomic and evolutionary theories are central to the contemporary scientific world-view, then consciousness falls into place naturally as an evolved phenotypic trait of certain types of organisms with highly developed nervous systems. I am not in this chapter concerned to defend this world view. Indeed, many thinkers whose opinions I respect, most notably Wittgenstein,

regard it as in varying degrees repulsive, degrading and disgusting. It seems to them to allow no place—or at most a subsidiary place—for religion, art, mysticism, and "spiritual values" generally. But like it or not, it is the world view we have. Given what we know about the details of the world—about such things as the position of elements in the periodic table, the number of chromosomes in the cells of different species, and the nature of the chemical bond—this world view is not an option. It is not simply up for grabs along with a number of competing world views. Our problem is not that we have somehow failed to come up with a convincing proof of the existence of God or that the hypothesis of an afterlife remains in serious doubt, it is rather that in our deepest reflections we cannot take such opinions seriously. When we encounter people who claim to believe such things, we may envy them the comfort and security they claim to derive from these beliefs, but at bottom we remain convinced that either they have not heard the good news or they are in the grip of faith. We remain convinced that somehow they must separate their minds into separate compartments to believe such things. When I lectured on the mind-body problem in India and was assured by several members of my audience that my views must be mistaken, because they personally had existed in their earlier lives as frogs or elephants, etc., I did not think "Here is evidence for an alternative world view" or even "Who knows, perhaps they are right" and my insensitivity was much more than mere cultural provincialism: Given what I know about how the world works, I could not regard their views as serious candidates for truth. And once you accept our world-view the only obstacle to granting consciousness its status as a biological feature of organisms is the outmoded dualistic/materialistic assumption that the "mental" character of consciousness makes it impossible for it to be a "physical" property. (Searle 1992, 90–91)

. . .

Anyone who has had even a modicum of "scientific" education after about 1920 should find nothing at all contentious or controversial in what I have just said. It is worth emphasizing also that all of this has been said without any of the traditional Cartesian categories. There has been no question of dualism, monism, materialism, or anything of the sort. Furthermore, there has been no question of "naturalizing consciousness"; it already is completely natural. Consciousness, to repeat, is a natural biological phenomenon. The exclusion of consciousness from the natural world was a useful heuristic device in the seventeenth century, because it enabled scientists to concentrate on phenomena that were measurable, objective and meaningless, that is, free of intentionality. But the exclusion was based on a falsehood. It was based on the false belief that consciousness was not part of the natural world. That single falsehood, more than anything else, more even than the sheer difficulty of studying consciousness with our available scientific tools has prevented us from arriving at an understanding of consciousness. (Searle 1992, 93; essentially identical assertion see Searle 2004, 111–13)

Searle's (1992) argument, then, for the claim that consciousness exists as a biological product of the brain, secreted by the brain in the same way a hormone is secreted by a gland, is then simply that is the only position consistent with a naturalistic world view in which what is known about the world is what we can get under the method of testing and confirmation in the natural sciences as we have come to know them.

Searle is quick to add that he is not interested in defending such a world view. He simply accepts it as obvious that it is our world view and asserts that the fact alone should be sufficient reason for the rest of us to accept it, and to make our philosophical explanations consistent with it (Searle 2004, 101). So, Searle urges that those who would affirm the existence of consciousness as a Cartesian immaterial substance, and thereby reject the biological nature of consciousness, disagree with our world view; and they thereby do so either because they are in the grip of religion or because they have not just yet heard the good news that science and the scientific world view is all we have when it comes to knowing anything about this world. "They either know nothing about science, or they are superstitious" (Searle 2004, 104ff).

COMMENTS ON SEARLE'S ARGUMENT

In assessing Searle's (1992; 2004) position, it is quite possible to accept a scientific world view, in any of the various ways that Searle may be inclined to define or to characterize it, and still, without being superstitious or essentially ignorant of natural science, to also reject Searle's biological construal of consciousness, simply because his position is purely philosophical, stipulative, and not in fact established in natural science. His position on the biological nature of consciousness contradicts his stated world view. After all, where in the scientific literature—biological, neurobiological, or otherwise—is it established either by observation or by the methods of testing and experiment, that consciousness is a biological property secreted by the brain in the same way a gland secretes a hormone? (Almeder 1994, 420–24).

Better yet, where in the history of science has it been established that consciousness exists, but cannot be a substance unlike any substance we ordinarily deal with in current physics or biology? In short, there is no scientifically well-confirmed (much less robustly confirmed) belief within science that consciousness is a biological product or a feature of the brain. We do not see the brain excrete consciousness in the same way we see a gland excrete a hormone. Consciousness is nothing like a hormone.

When this last objection is noted, Searle's (1992; 2004) materialist fallback position is that nevertheless the biological construal of consciousness is the only position consistent with our scientific world view.

Supposing indeed that to be the case, where was that world view established as a truth or as a robustly confirmed hypothesis in science? Besides that, what exactly does Searle mean by "our scientific world view"? Well, of course, he said above that adopting the scientific world view is just another way of saying that in the interest of attaining human knowledge we need to naturalize everything and take the methods of science as the only path to human knowledge.

But that is just a bit too vague because the concept of a scientific world view admits of no fewer than three logically distinct characterizations and, depending on which characterization one chooses, one may or may not have a justification for adopting a scientific world view; and one can argue that the only viable characterization of a "scientific world view" that is harmless, is the one that leaves it an open question as to what the nature of consciousness might turn out to be.

Incidentally, there are no fewer than three logically distinct forms of naturalized epistemology: (a) The only legitimately answerable questions about this world are those we can answer by appealing to the methods of testing and of confirmation in the natural sciences, and the only correct answers we have are those provided by natural science (replacement thesis); (b) There are legitimately answerable questions outside of natural science, but whether anybody knows anything or not is an empirical or scientific question (transformational thesis); and (c) The methods of the natural sciences is the only reliable method for acquiring a public understanding of the nature of the observed regularities and properties of the physical world (Almeder 1998).[1]

Finally, Searle (1992; 2004) apparently believes that simply because we have adopted a scientific world view (in some sense suitably explicated), then whether anybody likes it or not, that is a good reason for adopting it. Given all this, and when all the appeals to obviousness are done, the ultimately nagging question is why should anybody take seriously the biologizing of consciousness as something warranted in science or even as something warranted in terms of accepting a scientific world view?

Searle's (1992) argument that science has shown that consciousness, like any mental state, is a biological property of the brain and hence dies with the death of the brain. But it is by no means as obvious as he contends. Indeed, it is false that science has shown as much. Nobody, as we remarked above, has yet seen consciousness secreted by the brain in the way one can see a hormone secreted by a gland. It is also false that science has shown that consciousness cannot be some sort of Cartesian immaterial substance irreducible radically to any property of the brain.

Moreover, even if Searle's biologizing of consciousness and all other mental states were the only position consistent with accepting our scientific world view, Searle's refusal to defend such a world view reveals at best a lack of understanding of those arguments already in the literature to the effect that naturalizing everything (under either the replacement thesis or the transformation thesis) is fraught with difficulties, and at worst an elementary *ad populum* (an appeal to the general population).

There are other problems with Searle's proposed solution to the mind-body problem. He asserts, for example, that materialism and traditional dualism are false, that is, it is false that only material objects exist (because there are mental states) and it is false that traditional dualism is true (because that implies that there are substances not reducible to physical objects). For Searle, the trick is to realize that there are mental states and consciousness, but that they are in fact material or biological states of the system produced by the brain (Searle 1992, 15; Searle 2004, 110–13).

But demonstrably that is just neo-classical materialism. How this differs from the original form of eliminative materialism offered by Richard Rorty (1965) in his essay "Mind-Body Identity, Privacy, and Categories," is difficult to fathom. Searle's (1992) view is fundamentally that there are mental events, but they are material events, and this is clear if we can see that there is no disjunct between the mental and the material. Once we get over that hump, we will see that the original mind-body problem was generated by a bad definition of the mental and the material, one that made the mental and the material mutually exclusive.

WE DO NOT NEED CARTESIAN MINDS

We Need Only Physical Laws and Physical Properties

The fourth core objection reductive materialists frequently urge is that we simply have no need for Cartesian minds to explain anything, including human behavior. We only need physical laws and physical objects to explain and to predict all of human behavior; and even if we cannot now predict all of human behavior, at least it is something we can do in principle.

THE PRINCIPLE OF PARSIMONY AND REFLECTIONS ON CONSCIOUSNESS

This common objection feeds upon the traditional Principle of Parsimony. The Principle of Parsimony asserts that the only justification we have for believing in the existence of anything is that the belief explains something we could not otherwise explain equally well without that belief. Bypassing certain questions about what would count as an adequate theory for the explanation of human behavior, and whether the ability to predict human behavior in itself would count for such an explanation, this objection is, more than anything else, a challenge to the Cartesian dualist, to come up with good reasons for supposing that we need something more, or that there is something fundamentally wrong with commonly proposed explanations put forth by reductive materialists to explain human behavior. Here begins the trench warfare.

Take, for example, the problem of consciousness. Consciousness certainly does not seem to be a property like any other physical property. Everybody seemingly admits that it exists, but being generally aware of things is not like any other physical property we know about, or whose existence can be directly or indirectly inferred from observation of other physical properties.

Reductive materialists, however, will usually argue that being in a particular brain state is just being conscious; certain describable neurobiological activities always occur when consciousness is present, but are not there when consciousness is not present (Dennett 1991). Less popularly, as we saw above in the words of Searle (1992), other reductive materialists will argue that being conscious does not reduce simply to being in a particular brain state describable simply in neurochemistry, but rather reduces to being a biological property produced or secreted by the brain. We need not repeat the above reasons why the latter form of reductionism is unsatisfactory.

But the idea that consciousness is just being in a particular neurobiological state, complex or otherwise, which is the awareness we experience, as materialists say, does not seem to the Cartesian dualist to be any more empirically confirmed than alternative explanations such as the position offered above by Searle, or that offered by others who might urge that consciousness is neither a physical property nor any other empirically describable state of the brain. Rather, when consciousness is present certain parts of the brain light up, as it were, and would not light up otherwise because that is the way in which consciousness causes the brain to do the work it does in producing various human behaviors, such as believing, desiring, intending, remembering, loving, hating, and knowing. Further, as we shall see, there are other human behaviors that we cannot explain simply by some appeal to causal brain states as either causative or constitutive of such behavior.

COULD CARTESIAN IMMATERIAL SUBSTANCES EXPLAIN ANYTHING?

Examining Two Objections to a Negative Response

Some reductive materialists will now affirm, however, that the basic problem with the latter sorts of alternative hypotheses offered by Cartesians is that they cannot in principle provide an explanation for any human behavior because they exist as nomological danglers; they cannot serve as causes in any adequate explanation of human behavior. This is the fifth core objection to a Cartesian mind-body dualism wherein mental events are seen as causes of overt behavior.

This objection to Cartesian dualism has an enduring history. It survives on the principle that anything that will serve as a cause to explain observable human behavior will need to function by way of conveying kinetic energy from one physical object to another. Otherwise there would be no explanation for the human behavior that occurs because we would not be able to predict the behavior under the cause. If Cartesian immaterial substance could be a cause, they say, then something could occur without the transfer of kinetic energy, and as this well-known anti-Cartesian objection goes, that violates the Principle of Conservation of Energy, as it would allow for the overall increase of energy in the universe, just as if physical events could cause mental events then there would be an overall decrease in energy in the universe.

However seductive this last objection to belief in the existence of Cartesian immaterial substances, it suffers at least two fundamental flaws. The first is that the concept of a cause to which the reductive materialist appeals here begs the question in favor of his position that only physical objects exist, because they define a cause not simply as that object whose efficient action brings about a change in another object, but rather that object or force by whose conveyance of kinetic energy brings about another proportional and predictable change in the observable properties of the other object. When one defines causality in this way under the rubric of operationalizing basic concepts in science, the definition assumes that causality is a relationship between physical objects and is determinably present only when there is a transfer of kinetic energy in the way understood by traditional physics. This begs the question in favor of a concept of causality that obtains only between physical objects as we know them, and thus begs the question against any causal relation between a physical object and a Cartesian immaterial substance.

This then also begs the question in favor of mechanistic explanations of human behavior to the extent that that concept of causality is also implied in mechanistic explanations. The Anti-Cartesian would respond predictably, then, that the Cartesian dualist is unfortunately asking us to consider seriously the proposition that we cannot have explanations of human behavior (however much success we might have in predicting human behavior) in the natural sciences as we know them. Materialists may think that this last response closes the debate, because it is hard to take seriously anybody who thinks that natural science cannot provide us with any explanations of human behavior.

C. D. Broad's Defense Against Reductive Materialists

But what if Cartesian dualists are willing to accept that particular conclusion and relegate natural science to securing causal explanations among physical objects requiring the transfer of kinetic energy, and then reserve explanations of human behavior for a different type of causal interaction, namely, a basically primitive one wherein there is in fact a transfer of efficient energy between mental and physical objects, but not to be understood in terms of a transfer of kinetic energy between two typically observable physical objects? Science, as we currently understand it, may not be able to provide scientifically mature causal explanations of human behavior under this model, but it might still be able to predict a good deal of human behavior from many antecedent statistical correlations. Just as the unpredictable, at any moment, can and does occur but still has a cause, the predictable can and does occur without our being able to describe the cause in terms of a transfer of kinetic energy from one physical object to another. But, of course, at this point, the anti-Cartesian materialist may quite possibly continue to urge that we cannot then make any scientific sense of a causal relationship between the physical and the nonphysical, and that the supposition to the contrary is somehow incoherent.

On this last point, in an effort to establish the claim that it is neither logically impossible nor factually impossible that there can be a causal relations between physical objects and Cartesian immaterial substances, C. D. Broad (1962) in his *Lectures on Psychical Research*, once asked us to reflect on our own behaviors and experience of causality (96ff). When I raise my arm, for example, just after saying "I will now raise my arm," we usually explain the arm going up by saying "He raised his arm because he intended to raise his arm." The Anti-Cartesian materialist will not deny such common sense explanations, but he will add that wanting, loving, hating, knowing, believing, and intending, must be construed as causal agents identical to certain brain states that cause the arm to go up; it is just a case of brain-body interaction and there is nothing particularly mysterious here. Broad, however, might have pressed the issue further.

Why, one could ask, does my arm go up just after I say it will, or, better yet, why does the brain cause the arm to go up at that time and at no other time, than just after I say "I will now raise my arm"? What causes the brain to function as such an effective cause at that point and not before or after? If my arm went up autonomically, as a result of some neurological glitch, twitch, or some sort of chemical imbalance, we would not say "I raised my arm." What caused the brain to be in precisely the position it needs to be to cause the arm to go up at precisely that time when I say "I will now raise my arm" . . . and when I do not intend to raise it, or do not want to raise it, why is the brain state not then causing the arm to go up? If the answer here is that there is some other complex, or even some simple brain state that is at work to cause the brain to raise the arm, then the question will be, why does that particular cause of the brain activity occur at that time and at no other time?

And so we have to go into an infinite regress to explain why my arm is caused to go up by the brain at precisely that time when I say I will raise it and do raise it. This is problematic for any proposed causal explanation in terms of intentions and of wants that are presumptively reducible to brain or neuro-biological states. For the Cartesian, such a problem leads to the view that there are Cartesian immaterial substances causally responsible for human behavior.

To be told repeatedly, however, that there could not be such causes of human behavior because we would not understand in science how they work, is simply (again) to beg the question against their existence when there is good reason to think that the reductivist thesis fails to explain something as simple and as important as intentional acts like deliberately raising one's arm at a particular time.

Our not knowing in natural science how such causes work does not imply that there are no such causes, but only that we cannot understand them if we construe them in terms of a transfer of kinetic energy between two fundamentally physical objects as we ordinarily understand them operationally in scientific contexts.

Indubitably, the Cartesian dualist will claim that we are dealing here with some fundamentally different kind of causation between two different types of objects, although mental events and physical events will obviously need to have something very much in common for them to be enough alike for there to be any causal interaction at all.

CONCLUSION: REJECTING THE CORE
OBJECTIONS OF REDUCTIVE MATERIALISM

In Joseph Levine's (2001) excellent book *Purple Haze: The Puzzle of Consciousness*, he is right to have said that the antinomy in discussions on the problem of consciousness is that consciousness seems to be so basically irreducible to some interesting physical or material property and yet at the same time we feel the need for causal explanations which belief in irreducible consciousness undermines. This tension goes to the heart of the mind-body problem. The Cartesian mind-body dualist cannot help but be attentive to that antinomy.

But if what we have just argued above is reasonably persuasive in funding a rejection to core objections to Cartesian mind-body dualism, then we do not need to give up the thesis that Cartesian immaterial substances exist and are causes of human behavior. We only need to give up the idea that we can provide causal explanations of human behavior simply in terms of causes understood mechanistically or in terms of the transfer of kinetic energy as we usually understand it.

There may be important why-questions about human behavior, questions we cannot answer by appeal to the methods of testing and of confirmation in natural science as we currently understand them. If that is true, it raises serious further questions about the science of psychology, and whether it is really explaining human behavior, rather than using statistical correlations to successfully predict a good deal of human behavior. The latter, of course, is profoundly important and useful without our having to claim we are therein advancing causal explanations of human behavior.[2]

NOTES

1. For a full discussion of all three and an endorsement of (3), see Almeder 1998.

2. Dennett (1991) *Consciousness Explained* is in fact no different from that form of eliminative materialism that falls under the contingent identity thesis; see also Almeder 1992.

Chapter 2

Evidence Favoring Cartesian Mind-Body Dualism and Reincarnation

THE CASE FOR PERSONAL REINCARNATION

The *reincarnation hypothesis* examined in the following pages embraces only the following description and whatever it implies:

However we characterize it, there is something essential to some humans that we cannot justifiably describe as an observable physical object. It is not a physical property of any brain state. It is not a functional property of the brain. It is not demonstrably a biological property produced or caused by the brain. After biological death, this irreducible, essential property sometimes persists for some time, in some way, in some place, and for some reason or other, existing independently of the person's former brain and body. It is also the repository of certain personal memories and other mental or character traits irreducible to any biological properties or properties of the brain. It retains after death some of the personal memories the former person had before death and, for some reason or other, by some basic causal mechanism or other, it comes to reside in the fetus of a woman either at conception, or at some time during gestation, at birth, or shortly after birth.

Call this the *Minimalist Reincarnation Hypothesis*. The central question here before us is whether this hypothesis, as characterized, is demonstrably true. We call this a "minimalist hypothesis" because it tells us very little about the nature of this mysterious non-physical property or *stuff so essential to some people. We often think of this "stuff" as some species of a Cartesian "immaterial substance" having certain cognitive, volitional, and emotive characteristics (*Descartes 1985).

This minimalist hypothesis does not assert or imply that all human beings reincarnate at some time or other. We have no solid, empirical evidence for that claim. This empirical hypothesis does not profess to inform us why or how this process occurs, where this immaterial substance resides after death, and what it does before its reincarnation. Nor does it say how often this process of reincarnation occurs and whether there is some definite end to the process. The above hypothesis does not imply that every aspect of each human reincarnates whenever that person reincarnates, but only what is essential to the personality in question, namely only that which would be empirically sufficient to identify the person as distinct from any other person.

Historically, this minimalist construal of personal reincarnation is reminiscent of the ancient Pythagorean and Platonic conception of personality and it rejects bodily continuity as a necessary condition for personal identity. It is also consistent with Aristotelian conceptions of personality that *may* require bodily continuity as essential for human personality (Almeder 1998).

Under the above brief characterization, we may be more than what survives biological death, but what does survive is essential to some persons, and sufficient to distinguish those persons from any other person that might have existed as a human. What survives here is ostensibly not a physical object. Physicalists (reductive materialists) believe, without sufficient justification, that the only objects in this world are physical objects governed by the general laws of physics. They also believe that the universe has no center and has no edges.

In any event, as we will see in the following pages, the most important feature of this minimalist reincarnation hypothesis is that *it is, empirically testable, falsifiable, and confirmed as the best available empirical explanation for the relevant data in a number of careful case studies of people who claim to be reincarnated.*

Not unexpectedly, many people will reject outright the belief in personal reincarnation, even as an empirically verifiable hypothesis. They believe rather that the belief in reincarnation is basically a religious belief of some sort, or a bit of philosophical gibberish, or superstitious hocus-pocus. Some even believe that the hypothesis is absurd, worthy of ridicule, and incoherent to the core. Very few will probably believe that it might be empirically verifiable under the methods of testing and of confirmation in the natural sciences, much less *de facto* confirmed empirically. Be that as it may, we will examine and confront the salient objections to the minimalist reincarnation hypothesis, after presenting the basic argument for it.

WE CAN BEGIN WITH THE FOLLOWING THOUGHT EXPERIMENT:

Caesar on a Park Bench

The Thought Experiment

Imagine that you are sitting alone on a park bench reading a newspaper when a stranger approaches and sits beside you. Shortly thereafter the stranger interrupts your reading, and casually informs you that incidentally he is Julius Caesar reincarnated. Suppose further after that he tells you that he has several *personal* memories that only Julius Caesar had, but before he begins to list some of them, you interrupt him with the assertion that if he *really* is Julius Caesar in a different body, he needs to furnish you with some evidence by way of providing precise and verifiable *personal* memories that *only* Julius Caesar could have had. He agrees. You suspect, of course, that he may well be just a disheveled neurotic out for a nice day in the park.

The stranger then launches into his articulate narrative stating that he remembers having had an identical twin brother named Virgilius whom he loved. But for some unknown reason his parents secretly locked Virgilius in the wine cellar under the family villa near the Rubicon River where he and his brother often played as youths. Thereafter, he never saw Virgilius again. His parents never talked about his brother. He also says that much later, and before he crossed the Rubicon in 49 BC to invade Rome with his army, he wrote a short message to his missing twin brother just in case he, Julius Caesar, was killed in battle in Rome.

He clearly remembers writing this message to Virgilius telling him that if things went badly in Rome, he should take the fifty gold minted coins buried in a sack about ten feet deep and forty paces west of the familiar big rock beside the Rubicon, about a mile from the family villa. He tells you he also included the message with the newly minted gold coins, and he signed it with brotherly affection. He also tells you that he ordered his most trusted centurion, Cratylus Maximus to search secretly and exhaustively to make certain that if Virgilius is still alive anywhere, Virgilius inherits the sack of gold coins if he, Julius Caesar, is killed in Rome. He, the stranger beside you, also remembers now that Quintus was killed in the battle and so Virgilius never got the message or the gold coins. By the way, the stranger also speaks fluently Ciceronian Latin and plays well an ancient Roman lyre—neither of which skill could he have learned in this life for obvious reasons.

Now suppose that, for whatever reason, you decided to investigate this strange narrative, and so you went a few weeks later to dig up the location described in the message allegedly sent by Caesar to his lost twin brother. Before the digging you hired five distinguished archeologists who had certified in writing that the ground down at least twenty feet had not been disturbed since 49 BC. You then dug several feet down and unearthed a sack containing fifty new Roman gold coins along with the letter signed and dated by Caesar.

After an exhaustive search of all possible public records, you found no official or historical records that Caesar's mother ever had identical twin boys. No official records anywhere in the Roman Empire could be found to the effect that these identical twins existed. Several distinguished historians searched far and wide, night and day, but found no mention anywhere of an identical twin named Virgilius born to Julius Caesar's mother. But at the back of the family villa near the Rubicon you finally found a few months later a moss-covered, barely visible, old stone inscribed with the single word "Virgilius" engraved on it.

After that, you also hired some famous graphologists to examine the letter allegedly signed by Julius Caesar. After a careful reading, those graphologists certified, along with several other independent expert graphologists, that the handwriting in the message was undeniably the handwriting of Julius Caesar.

Several months later you learned that an elderly lady in Sicily discovered in her attic a box containing barely readable family records, handed down from generation to generation, in which the mother of Julius Caesar wrote that her famous son Julius had an identical twin named Virgilius who was buried at the back of the family villa property near the Rubicon River. Period.

THIS ENDS OF FIRST THOUGHT EXPERIMENT

The Question

If you were the investigator in the above thought experiment, would you now accept the stranger's claim that he is indeed Julius Caesar reincarnated?

Is it really *possible* that this stranger on the park bench could be Julius Caesar reincarnated? After all, you empirically confirmed the stranger's personal memories as reliable memories that *only Julius Caesar could have had, and you would have verified those memories, not as quasi-memories* but as true or apparent memories that nobody else could have had except Julius Caesar. The stranger on the park bench certainly could not have acquired those personal memories of events in his current life. In short, how would you explain his having the confirmed memories of Julius Caesar, reliable memories that he could not have acquired in this life, if he was not Julius Caesar reincarnated?

If the stranger on the park bench had similar memories that only Julius Caesar could have had, then it seems only natural to believe that the stranger really is, as he claimed to be, Julius Caesar reincarnated, because that is arguably the best currently available explanation of his knowing what only Julius Caesar could have known. How could we certify another person's demonstrably true memories about events he could not have witnessed in this life (and which nobody else knew) and not be that other person while claiming to be Julius Caesar reincarnated?

Doubtless, there are critics who will object that there are, or there must be, other ways to explain how one might have the personal memories of another person long dead without being that person. Some philosophers, indeed, will *prefer* a different explanation of the data to the effect that some people might have mysterious ways of *picking up* personal memories of other persons long dead without being those persons (see Ayer 1956).[1] But that is not an explanation. More on this later. Turn now to our second and last thought experiment. It is similar.

THE SECOND THOUGHT EXPERIMENT

In his excellent book, *Reasons and Persons*, the distinguished philosopher Derek Parfit (1984) challenged anybody who claims "that the concept of a Cartesian Ego (or an immaterial spiritual substance frequently referred to as a soul or a discarnate person) is unintelligible, impossible, or incoherent" (227). As we noted in chapter 1, Parfit seriously doubts that view. He believes rather that there *might have been* evidence supporting the Cartesian view. For example, he asserts that:

> There might, for example, have been evidence supporting the belief in reincarnation. One piece of such evidence might be this. A Japanese woman might claim to remember living a life as a Celtic hunter and warrior in the Bronze Age. On the basis of her apparent memories, she might make many predictions that could be checked by archaeologists. Thus, she might claim to remember having a bronze bracelet, shaped like two fighting dragons. And she might claim that she remembers burying this bracelet beside some particular megalith, just before the battle in which she was killed. Archaeologists might now just find such a bracelet buried in this spot, and their instruments might show that the earth had not been disturbed for at least 2,000 years. The Japanese woman might make many other such predictions, all of which are verified. (Parfit 1984, 227)

Parfit continues asking us to imagine that there are countless other cases in which people alive today claim to remember living certain past lives that provide similar predictions that are all verified. Suppose also that countless numbers of other people have similar memories and provide similar stories over time that are robustly verified or confirmed. If there was enough such evidence, *and if* there was no other way in which we could explain how most of us could know such detailed facts about the distant past, we might have to conclude that the Japanese woman has a way of knowing about the life of a Celtic Bronze Age warrior which is like her memory of her own life" (Parfit 1984, 227).

Parfit is certainly not arguing for the existence of Cartesian immaterial substances. He is simply arguing that *if* we had a case like the stranger on the park bench (a case in which the stranger has the personal memories that *only* the former person referenced could have had, and *if* we verified that the memory claims were true) then we might justifiably believe that the stranger was in fact the former person reincarnated.

A. J. Ayer (1956) would also agree, however, that "we might conclude not that reincarnation has occurred but that some people are able to acquire by some means or other the true memories of persons long since dead without being those persons reincarnated" (193–94). So both philosophers would apparently agree; however, that there are no such cases in evidence, although if there were, we would be rationally justified in accepting belief in personal reincarnation in such cases. But Ayer (and not Parfit) would certainly prefer rather to believe that some people are capable of acquiring memories of persons long since dead without being those persons.

One problem with Ayer's final position, incidentally, is that, apart from failing to justify his stated preference on the matter, he had earlier argued that if somebody had the true memories that *only* Julius Caesar could have had, that person could justifiably be accepted as Julius Caesar reincarnated, because for Ayer, along with so many others, *the criterion for personal identity is intuitively just the having of unique continuity of personal memories* (Ayer 1963). Under this popular criterion for personal identity, the stranger on the park bench would turn out to be Julius Caesar reincarnated, and certainly Ayer seems to have been tempted to accept the stranger as Julius Caesar reincarnated (see, for example, Broad 1962; Chalmers 1996; Levine 2001; Horgan, 2006; Swinburne 1984; Kim 2005).

By the way, Parfit ended up affirming that if I had the true memories that only the Japanese lady had, I would be the Bronze Age Warrior reincarnated who buried his dragon bracelet—provided many people had the same sort of confirmed memories, and provided we tested and responsibly rejected all the available competing explanations of how one could have memories that only Julius Caesar could have had without being Julius Caesar. That is what it would have taken to confirm empirically the existence of irreducible Cartesian immaterial substances.

PARFIT'S CONDITIONS

Problematically, Parfit's two added conditions (namely that there be many people who, over a long period of time, have had the same sort of experience, and that all plausible explanations outside of appealing to reincarnation for the data would be tested and refuted) are that those two conditions are not necessary for determining whether any particular person who claims to be the reincarnation of a person who lived earlier, is in fact that person. Again, why would it not be sufficient simply to show that the stranger on the park bench, for example, is indeed Julius Caesar just in case he demonstrably knows or remembers something that only Julius Caesar could have known? What better explanation could one offer for the data than that the stranger on the park bench is indeed Julius Caesar in a body different than the one Caesar had a long time ago? In any case, Parfit decided that there are, in fact, no such empirically confirmed cases, and so the discussion is moot or merely theoretical.

AYER AND PARFIT ACCEPT REINCARNATION AS VERIFIABLE

Certainly Ayer, Parfit, and others would be justified in asserting that reincarnation is, in principle, an empirically testable and verifiable hypothesis. After all, if one was in fact the reincarnation of Julius Caesar or a Bronze Age warrior that would imply and predict that they have demonstrable memories that only Julius Caesar or the Bronze Age warrior would have had. If the person claiming to be Caesar cannot provide us with the right observational data in terms of having personally witnessed some fact that to this day nobody (except him) knows anything about, and if that fact can be ascertained only now, we would have evidence that such memories are true and indicative of his being Julius Caesar. If some sensory fact is implied deductively from his memory claims about what happened long before he was born in his current body and was known only to him, then it should be easy to show that his memory claim was true and that only Julius Caesar would know about it.[2]

Before examining objections to the very idea of reincarnation, as an empirically verifiable and falsifiable hypothesis, first turn to a few well-known cases and types of cases in the research of Ian Stevenson, his colleagues, and others.

STEVENSON'S CRITERIA FOR AN IDEAL CASE

Dr. Ian Stevenson, M.D. was a distinguished psychiatrist who died in 2007 of pneumonia after more than forty years of focused research on reincarnation studies at the University of Virginia (UVA) School of Medicine. Before he began his research on reincarnation, he had served as a Distinguished University Professor and Chairman of the Department of Psychiatry in the UVA Medical School. Stevenson's (1978) most popular book, among many, remains *Twenty Cases Suggestive of Reincarnation*. His basic argument for the belief in personal reincarnation is simply that it offers the best available explanation of a substantial body of observable behavioral data that, until fairly recently, has largely been ignored or rejected for variously unacceptable reasons.

THE SIX CORE FEATURES LISTED

This body of data to which Stevenson (1978) refers consists of a number of case studies (described in detail in *Twenty Cases*, and elsewhere), which typically share at least the following six core features (see also Stevenson 1974; 1975; 1980; 1984; 2001):

1. A young person, usually between the ages of three and nine years old, claims to remember having lived an earlier life with a different name. In this case, a young boy provides a detailed description of his alleged earlier life, a description including, but not restricted to, where and when he lived, his name and the names and characteristics of his relatives, highly selective historical events that could be known only by the person he claims to have been in that earlier life, the way he lived and the specific details of the way in which he died.
2. These memory claims consist of two types: (a) Those that admit of simple verification in terms of available public information, and (b) Those admitting of verification but not in terms of currently available public information. (Stevenson 1978)

For example, if a young person from Evanston, Illinois, claims to remember having lived an earlier life as a person named Lazarus Smart, born July 17, 1630, in Boston, Massachusetts, as the son of Mary and Abraham Smart who lived on Boylston Street during the Great Boat Fire of 1642, then that one Lazarus Smart did in fact exist under this description could be verified easily in terms of available birth records, historical documents, and other information publicly accessible.

But if the same person claims to recall having secretly buried a silver spoon on which he carved the initials L. S. in the concrete pier under the Northwest Corner of the Boylston Street Church when it was being rebuilt in May of 1642, then that sort of claim would be verifiable and falsifiable, but not in terms of currently known or existing information.

3. The person claiming to remember having lived a past life is carefully interviewed, asked to provide detailed personal and private information one would expect him to have if he did live that earlier life as Lazarus Smart; and he provides such information.
4. Investigators independently confirm both sorts of memory claims and, in some cases (those cases in which the person's claims refer to extant family members with whom he was intimate), family members are

interviewed and confront the person who reminds them of various private details of the life they spent together.
5. The person claiming to remember having lived a past life may also manifest certain skills (such as speaking fluently a foreign language or dialect, or playing an instrument) that the alleged person in the earlier life had but which the person claiming to have lived an earlier life could not have acquired in this life. For example, if a person claims to have lived a life in eighteenth-century Sweden, and in a hypnotic trance then begins to speak and describe his earlier life in a difficult but clear dialect of eighteenth-century Swedish, that person (assuming we can document that he has not learned or been exposed to the study of eighteenth-century Swedish) manifests skills not acquired in this life. And finally,
6. The real possibility of deception, by way of fraud or of hoax on the part of the person claiming to have lived a past life, cannot now be substantiated.

Stevenson's basic argument is that for cases having characteristics of 1 through 6, the best available empirical explanation that plausibly fits the data supports belief in personal reincarnation. Opponents of reincarnation must provide an equally plausible or better alternative explanation for the data if they are to refute the belief in personal reincarnation. Before examining the strongest objections to what are compelling case studies, we can sketch some of what Stevenson regarded as what would be ideal cases *suggestive* of reincarnation.

STEVENSON'S RESERVATIONS AND THE IDEAL CASE

As is evident from the title *Twenty Cases Suggestive of Reincarnation*, Stevenson (1978) was reluctant to say that the cases he had examined *prove* the point. On the contrary, he believed that the argument for reincarnation would be won only by finding an *ideal case*, that is, one that meets the following eight conditions:

7. It is rich in verified memory claims that are not accountable in terms of Clairvoyance, ESP (telepathy), or Cryptomnesia.[3]
8. It is attended by the presence of a complicated skill (such as speaking a foreign language, or playing a musical instrument) that demonstrably could not have been learned by the subject in their present life, but which are demonstrably talents of the subject in the past life.
9. It is attended by appropriate birthmarks corresponding to wounds received in the earlier life remembered by the subject, and the occurrence of the wounds in the previous life is independently verified.
10. It is a case wherein the memory claims are not very much diminished with age, nor do they need to be induced under hypnotic trance or regression.

11. It is a case in which the subject's identification with a past personality is recognized by the subject as continuous with their present personality rather than substitutive of the present personality, and the identification is maintained over a long period of time—preferably into adulthood (Stevenson 1978, 145ff).[4]
12. It is a case in which the subject's identification with a past personality cannot be explained by the influence of parents or any other personality (Stevenson 1978, 359–60).
13. It is a case wherein the subject, as a result of their identification with a past personality, manifests predictable emotional responses to specific events and to persons remembered in the past life.
14. It is a case wherein the subject is recognized as the past person reincarnated, and is accepted over a long period of time by many extant family members or friends (who have nothing to gain by the recognition and acceptance) of the past personality. (See Stevenson, 1978, 145ff, 169ff, 359–60)

Most of the available cases that Stevenson and others have examined closely do not satisfy all of the eight conditions just specified. We will see shortly, however, that there is no need to satisfy all of these conditions in order to establish a very strong case of verified belief, as we would require of any empirical hypothesis. Before doing that, we can describe briefly a few of the standing cases and comment on them before going into the strongest objections to belief in reincarnation—as defined in minimalist terms noted above.

Unfortunately, space does not allow here for more than a few detailed compelling case studies. As you will see, like the thought experiments above, they all involve subjects claiming to be a certain person reincarnated and who has knowledge and memories of historical events known only by that person generally long since deceased. The people making the claim to be reincarnated know something that only the person in the former life could know. Remember that in the thought experiments above, the subjects had knowledge that only Caesar or only the Bronze Age warrior would have known, and if they had those confirmed memories their claims to be reincarnated stand as the best available explanation of how they could know what only the former person could know.

THE BISHEN CHAND CASE

Bishen Chand Kapoor was born in 1921 to the Gulham family living in the city of Bareilly in India. At about one and a half years of age, Bishen started asking questions about the town of Pilibhit, which was approximately fifty miles from Bareilly. Nobody in his family knew anybody in Pilibhit. Bishen

Chand asked to be taken there and it became obvious that he believed he had lived there during an earlier life (for case details see Stevenson 1975, 167ff).

As time passed, Bishen talked regularly of his earlier life there in Pilibhit. His family became increasingly distressed with his behavior. By the summer of 1926, when he was five and a half years old, Bishen claimed to remember his previous life quite clearly. He remembered that his name had been Laxmi Narain, and that he had been the son of a wealthy landowner. Bishen claimed to remember an uncle named Har Narain, who turned out to be Laxmi Narain's father. He also described the house in which he had lived, saying it included a shrine room and separate quarters for women. Frequently he had enjoyed singing and dancing with *nautsch* girls, professional dancers who also functioned as prostitutes. He remembered enjoying parties of this sort at the home of a neighbor, Sander Lal, who lived in "a house with a green gate" (Stevenson 1975, 165). Indeed, little Bishen Chand one day recommended to his father that he take on a mistress in addition to his wife.

Because Bishen's family was poor (his father was a government clerk), Bishen Chand's memories of an earlier and wealthier life only made him resentful of his present living conditions with the Gulham family. He sometimes refused to eat the food, complaining that even his servants would not eat such food.

One day Bishen's father mentioned that he was thinking of buying a watch and little Bishen Chand said: "Papa, don't buy. When I go to Pilibhit I shall get you three watches from a Muslim watch dealer whom I established there" (Stevenson 1975, 165). Then he provided the name of the dealer.

His sister Kamla, was three years older than he, and caught Bishen drinking brandy one day, which finally explained the dwindling amount of alcohol kept in the home for medical purposes only. In his typically superior way, the child told her that he was quite accustomed to drinking brandy. He drank a good deal of alcohol in his earlier life. Later he claimed to have had a mistress in his former life, again showing he knew the difference between a wife and a mistress. Her name, he said, was Padma.

Padma was a prostitute. Bishen considered her his exclusive property because he claimed to have killed a man he saw coming from her apartment. Bishen Chand's memory claims came to the attention of one K. K. N. Sahay, an attorney in Bareilly. Sahay went to the Kapoor home and recorded the surprising things the young boy was saying. Thereafter, he arranged to take Bishen Chand, along with his father and his older brother, to Pilibhit. Not quite eight years had elapsed since the death of Laxmi Narain, whom this little boy was claiming to have been in his earlier life.

Crowds were waiting when they arrived at Pilibhit. Nearly everyone in town had known of the wealthy family and its profligate member Laxmi Narain, who had been involved with the prostitute Padma (who still lived there) and who, in a jealous rage, had shot and killed a rival lover of Padma's. Although Laxmi Narain's family had been sufficiently influential to get the charges dropped, he died a few months afterward of natural causes at the age of thirty-two years.

When taken to Laxmi's old government school, Bishen Chand ran to where his classroom had been. Somebody produced an old picture and Bishen recognized in it some of Laxmi Narain's classmates, one of who happened to be in the crowd. When the classmate asked about their teacher, Bishen correctly described him as a fat, bearded man.

In the part of the town where Laxmi Narain had lived, Bishen Chand recognized the house of Sander Lal, the house that he had previously described, before being brought to Pilhibit, as having a green gate. The lawyer Sahay, when writing a report later for the national newspaper the *Leader*, in August 1926, claimed to have seen the gate himself and verified that the color was green. The boy also pointed to the courtyard where he said the *nautch* girls entertained with singing and dancing. Merchants in the area verified the boy's claims. In the accounts published by the *Leader*, Sahay noted that the name of the prostitute with whom the boy associated in his previous life was repeatedly sought by people in the crowd who were following the boy. When Bishen Chand mentioned the name "Padma," the people certified that the name was correct.

During that day, the boy was presented with a set of *tabla*, a pair of drums. The father said that Bishen had never seen *tabla* before, but to the surprise of his family and of all those assembled, Bishen Chand played them skillfully, as Laxmi Narain had done much earlier. When the mother of Laxmi Narain met Bishen, a strong attachment was immediately renewed between them. Bishen Chand answered the questions she asked, such as the time in his previous life when he had thrown out her pickles, and he successfully named and described Laxmi Narain's personal servant. He also gave the caste to which the servant belonged. He later claimed that he preferred Laxmi Narain's mother to his own.

Finally, Bishen Chand's older brother testified that Bishen could, when he was a child, read *Urdu*, written in Arabic script, before he had been taught this language. Bishen's father in a sworn statement about the case, stated that as a child, Bishen had used some Urdu words that he could not have learned in the family—words such as *masurate* (woman's quarters) and *kopal* (lock), rather than the usual Hindi words *zenana* and *tala*. Laxmi Narain was reasonably well educated and quite capable of speaking Urdu.

In commenting on this case, Stevenson said that it is especially significant because a reliable attorney kept an early record when most of the principals were still alive and capable of verifying Bishen Chand's memory claims (see Stevenson 1975, 176ff). Many of the people who knew Laxmi Narain were still alive and well when Bishen was making his claims. They verified nearly all of the statements Bishen made before he went to Pilibhit.

Moreover, according to Stevenson, the possibility of fraud is remote because Bishen Chand's family had little to gain from the association with the Laxmi Narain family (Stevenson 1975, 177). It was well known that the latter had become destitute after Laxmi Narain had died. As in most cases similar to this, the events could not be explained in terms of anticipated financial gain. Turn now to a second case.

THE MRS. SMITH CASE

In his book *The Cathars and Reincarnation*, a British psychiatrist named Dr. Arthur Guirdham (1970) describes in detail a case that compelled him to accept the belief in reincarnation. The woman in the case, Mrs. Smith, was his patient and he met her in 1961 when he was Chief Psychiatrist at Bath Hospital in England. Mrs. Smith's problem was that she had persistent nightmares during which she screamed so loudly that she and her husband feared it would wake the whole neighborhood. Guirdham examined her closely for neuroses but concluded that she had none. After a few months, Mrs. Smith told Guirdham that when she was a girl, she had written her dreams down. She had also written down things that came spontaneously to her mind as recollections—things she could not understand and that had to do with people and specific names she had never heard. She gave the papers to the doctor, and he examined them (Guirdham 1970, cited in Stevenson 1975, 108).

Guirdham was surprised to find that what she had written as a schoolgirl were verses of songs in medieval French and in *Lang d'Oc*, the language spoken in Southern France in the twelfth and thirteenth centuries. He ascertained that she had never studied these languages in school and that there was no source available to her for learning them. He sent a report of her story to Professor René Nelli of Toulouse and asked for the professor's opinion. Nelli responded that her writings gave an accurate account of the Cathars in Toulouse in the thirteenth century. The Cathars were a large group of Christian dissidents of the extreme dualist persuasion, whose religious beliefs were close to the Albigensians and centered on the belief in reincarnation. They were persecuted and destroyed during the Inquisition.

Only gradually did Mrs. Smith admit to having had an intensive increase of memories in her early teens—memories of a past life with a Cathar priest named Roger de Grisolles, whom she loved very much, and who taught her Cathar rituals and religious principles (Guirdham 1970, cited in Stevenson 1975, 10). Guirdham states that, apart from her dreams, Mrs. Smith had experienced a number of these spontaneous recollections, and she told, in horrid detail, her recollection of the massacre of the Cathars (Guirdham 1970, cited in Stevenson 1975, 73–74).

Mrs. Smith also told Guirdham that in her dreams and recollections of a previous life she had been kept prisoner in a certain church crypt. Guirdham notes that, at first, experts said that this church crypt had never been used for that purpose, but later research showed that on one occasion so many prisoners were taken that there was no room for all of them in regular prisons. Some had been kept in that very crypt.

Guirdham visited the south of France in 1967 to investigate the case. He read thirteenth-century manuscripts (available to only a limited number of scholars), and these manuscripts showed that Mrs. Smith's account was accurate. She had given Guirdham names and descriptions of people, places, and events, all of which turned out to be accurate down to the last detail. Guirdham claims that there was no normal way in which Mrs. Smith could have known about these things. He even found in the manuscripts four songs she wrote as a child. They were correct, word for word (Guirdham 1970, cited in Stevenson 1975, 125ff).

Guirdham (1970) notes that, although his subject claimed never to have read any books on the subject of thirteenth-century life, she made correct drawings of old French coins, jewelry worn at the time, and the layout of buildings—to say nothing about the intricate details of Cathar ritual.

Guirdham further attests that Mrs. Smith was able to name and to place accurately in their family and social relationships, people who do not appear in the textbooks, but who were ultimately traced by going back to the Dog Latin records of the Inquisition.

These minor characters are still traceable, owing to the antlike industry of Inquisitors and their clerks. Mrs. Smith remembered members of the Fanjeaux and Mazzarolles families, in particular giving their first names and the roles they played. She recollected treating her dear friend Roger de Grisolles with sugarloaf as a tonic.

However, the expert called this into question: the existence of sugar at this time in Europe was doubted. Further investigation disclosed that sugar in loaf form was derived from Arab medicine, and did indeed exist at this period in France (Guirdham 1970, cited in Stevenson 1975, 9).

Even more remarkable was Mrs. Smith's description of her death when she was burned at the stake. This event she both dreamed and subsequently claimed to remember. The description, sent by Guirdham (1970) as part of his case, read as follows:

> The pain was maddening. You should pray to God when you are dying, if you can pray when you are in agony. In my dream I did not pray to God . . . I didn't know when you were burnt to death you'd bleed. I thought the blood would all

dry up in the terrible heat. But I was bleeding heavily. The blood was dripping and hissing in the flames. I wished I had enough blood to put the flames out. The worst part was my eyes. I hate the thought of going blind. . . . In this dream I was going blind. I tried to close my eyelids but I couldn't. They must have been burnt off, and now those flames were going to pluck out my eyes with their evil fingers. The flames weren't so cruel after all, they began to feel cold. Icy cold. It occurred to me that I wasn't burning to death but freezing to death. I was numb with the cold and suddenly I started to laugh. I had fooled those people who thought they could burn me. I am a witch. I had magiked [*sic*] the fire and turned it to ice. (Guirdham 1970, cited in Stevenson 1975, 89)

Finally, in a lecture titled "Reincarnation and the Practice of Medicine," given in London, March 1969, Guirdham (1970) reflected on certain crucial details of the case, many of which were discussed in his book:

Twenty-five years ago, as a student, a schoolgirl at the age of 13, she was insisting the Cathar priests did not always wear black. You will find the statement that they did in any book on the subject until 1965. Yet she said that her friend in the thirteenth century wore dark blue. It now transpires that at one sitting of the Inquisition [the inquisition of Jacques Fournier, who was bishop at Palmiers] it came out ten times in one session that Cathar priests sometimes wore dark blue or dark green. But that fact has been lying in the archives in Latin for long enough, and was only accessible to the public since 1965 when Duvernoy edited the record of the said inquisitors that was published in Toulouse in 1966. But this woman knew this in 1944 as a girl.

Again she could describe rituals in a house, a kind of convent. . . . Professor Nelli, the greatest living authority on the Troubadors—who definitely are connected with the Cathars—wrote to me and said:

"This is almost exactly Cathar rituals, making allowance for local deviation."

He also added later that he could tell me where the place was, the Convent of Montreal. By way of future advice, he added that, in case of doubt, one should "go by the patient." Professor Nelli is the most meticulous and skeptical assessor of evidence.

When I first wrote to another specialist, Professor Duvernoy of Toulouse, he said, "Get in touch with me about anything you want. I am astonished at your detailed knowledge of Catharism." I couldn't say "I've got this by copying down the dreams of a woman of thirty-six or seven which she had when she was a grammar school girl of thirteen." He's found out since, but he is all the more keen to supply me with the evidence. (Guirdham 1970, 140)

LET US TURN TO ANOTHER INTERESTING CASE.

The Lydia Johnson Case

Xenoglossy refers to an alleged ability to speak—and often also to understand—a foreign language that has not been learned by the speaker in any normal way. This phenomenon has occurred in cases similar to the past two cases, and constitutes a special kind of evidence in favor of reincarnation—evidence beyond that offered by memory of people and places and acquired skills.

In Stevenson's books (1974; 1984) *Xenoglossy* and *Unlearned Language*, Stevenson offers us the Case of Lydia Johnson, and the Case of Gretchen. After an overview of these two cases, we will launch into examining the major objections to the possibility of personal reincarnation.

In 1973, Lydia Johnson agreed to help her husband with his experiments in hypnotism. She was an excellent subject because she could easily slip into a deep trance. Dr. Harold Johnson (not his real name) was a respected Philadelphia physician. He had taken up hypnotism in 1971 to help some of his patients with the treatments they were receiving. His experiments with his wife worked quite well so he decided to try a regression on his wife, taking her back in time. In the middle of the regression she flinched (as if struck) and screamed. She clutched her head, and he ended the regression immediately. Unfortunately, his wife had a headache that would not cease. Twice Johnson repeated the session and the result was the same. Each time Lydia awoke from the trance, she said she had visualized a scene with water in which old people seemed to be forced into it to drown. She had the sense of being pulled down, and then the blow, her scream, and then her headache. As a result of all this, Johnson then called in another hypnotist, one Dr. John Brown (not his real name). Brown repeated the session but before the pain could occur again, he told her "You are ten years younger than that." And then it happened.

She began to talk in words and in occasional phrases. Some of it was in broken English, but much of it was in a foreign language that nobody at the session could understand. Her voice was deep and masculine. Then from the mouth of this thirty-seven-year-old housewife came the words "I am a man." When asked her name, she said "Jensen Jacoby." It was in this session (and in other that followed) that she told in her low masculine voice of living in a small village in Sweden some three centuries ago.

These sessions were tape-recorded and careful notes were kept. Swedish linguists were called in to translate Jensen's statements. In the later sessions he spoke a language totally foreign to Lydia. When asked "What do you do for a living?" He answered in eighteenth-century Swedish, "a farmer." Where do you live?" He answered "In the house" and when asked "Where is the house?" he answered again in Swedish, "In Hansen." These questions were asked in Swedish (Stevenson 1984, 3).

Judging by what Jensen said, he had a simple personality, quite consistent with the peasant life he described. He showed little knowledge of anything beyond his own village, and a trading center he visited. He raised cows, horses, goats, and chickens. He ate goat's cheese, bread, milk, salmon, and poppy seed cakes made by his wife Latvia. He had built his own stone house and he was one of three sons. He and Latvia had no children. He had run away from home. His mother had been a Norwegian.

Certain objects were brought in while Lydia was entranced. She was asked to open her eyes and identify the object. As Jensen, she had identified a model of a seventeenth-century Swedish ship which she correctly identified in Swedish; so too a wooden container used then for measuring grain, a bow and arrow, and poppy seeds. She did not, however, know how to use modern tools—for example, pliers (Stevenson 1984, 10).

All the data in this case came from Jensen's statements and associated behavior. The principal investigator was Ian Stevenson, who also provided the written narrative of this case and the next case, The Gretchen Case.

THE GRETCHEN CASE

Similar to the Lydia Johnson (*qua* Jensen) case is the Gretchen case. The responsive Xenoglossy was induced by hypnosis. After periods of an hour or so, the communicating personalities were dismissed by the hypnotist; and in both cases, while communicating personalities could speak their languages responsively, they did so only haltingly and with imperfect grammar and vocabulary. Ian Stevenson began to investigate the Gretchen Case in 1971 (Stevenson 1984, chap. 1).

In the late 1960s, Carroll Jay (hereafter C. J.), who was a Methodist minister and a hypnotist, began experimenting with suggestions that his subjects should regress to "previous lives." One day, C. J. hypnotized his wife Dolores (hereafter D. J.) in order to relieve her from a backache. In the course of doing this, he asked her if her back hurt. She responded "Nein." This occurred on May 10, 1970. Three days later, on May 13, he hypnotized her again and the new trance personality identified herself by saying "Ich bin Gretchen" (I am Gretchen). Over the next few months further sessions were held, and Gretchen gradually emerged more fully and gave more details about herself. Stevenson noted that, with but rare exceptions, Gretchen spoke only German words. Both of the Jays stated that—other than the few words that every American knows—they knew absolutely no German at the time the case developed. Naturally then C. J. did not understand any of what Gretchen was saying. But with the help of a dictionary and some friends who knew some German, Stevenson gradually began to piece together the story Gretchen was relating. Gretchen understood simple English, and initially she would answer in German the questions put to her in English. Shortly thereafter she began to answer in German questions put to her in German.

The sessions were taped beginning on August 2, 1970; Stevenson (1984) offers a verbatim transcript of the extracts from the tapes in his book *Unlearned Language* (transcript, appendix B).

Stevenson had heard of the case in 1971; and in September, accompanied by a companion, he traveled to Mount Horab in Ohio where the Jays lived. During a number of subsequent sessions in which the Gretchen personality emerged, Stevenson had sensible conversations with her in German, as did a number of other people who were native German speakers or who were conversant in the spoken language. With one exception (a woman who wanted to leave up to the reader of the transcripts in question whether Gretchen really understood what she said), the general conclusion accepted by all who spoke German with Gretchen was that, although sometimes she did not respond at all well to questions asked in German, nonetheless she spoke German responsively and answered quite satisfactorily some questions put to her in that language.[5]

In seeking to determine whether D. J., or Gretchen, might have learned her German in ordinary ways, Stevenson (1984) examined the early lives of C. J. and D. J. He searched for any opportunity that D. J. might have had for learning German—"perhaps adventitiously" when she was young (9). With the approval of the Jays, Stevenson spent two days in Clarksburg, West Virginia, where the Jays had grown up and where members of D. J.'s family were still living. C. J. provided Stevenson with the names of people who would be qualified informants on the important question of his wife's exposure to the German language spoken during her childhood. Stevenson interviewed all those whose names had been given to him.

Moreover, he took the precaution of browsing in the neighborhood where D. J. had spent her childhood, and interviewed a number of people whose names C. J. had not given to him. He interviewed nineteen persons in Clarksburg and some of its adjoining suburbs. He also corresponded in 1973 with Dorothy Davis (1970), author of *History of Harrison County, West Virginia*, concerning the settlement of German-speaking immigrants in the area of Clarksburg, which is the county seat and principal town of Harrison County.

Further, on February 5, 1974, D. J. took a polygraph test for lie detection with regard to her knowledge of the German language. The test was administered by a Mr. Richard Arther in his offices in New York City. According to D. J. and C. J., no one had spoken German to Gretchen or to D. J. before the session on May 10, 1971. Stevenson noted that after a few more sessions with the Gretchen-personality—this time at the UVA—Mrs. Jay, understandably exhausted, wanted no more experiments. She and her husband had undergone a good number of them already, and were receiving adverse criticism from the community where they lived, who thought the experiments were (as Stevenson related) "to put it mildly, outside what might be expected of a Christian clergyman and his wife" (Stevenson 1984, 11). In 1977, C. J. published an account of the case in which he described some problems he and his family endured during and after its development. Apart from the time spent in the actual sessions with Gretchen, and in transcribing the tapes, Stevenson estimates that the interviews with the Jays on various aspects of the case lasted about twenty-five hours.

In conveying the results of the investigation into whether D. J. could have acquired her knowledge of German through normal processes, Stevenson established that no school D. J. had ever attended taught German, no family members (even grandparents) ever spoke German, and nobody in her neighborhood ever spoke German. She married right after high school, at eighteen years of age, and settled down in the same town. Further, as Stevenson documented, the lie detector test on D. J. supported her claim that neither she nor her husband had ever studied or knew any German. Lastly, it was also clear that up until the development of the case, the Jays had nothing more than what would be described as an intelligent layman's interest in paranormal phenomena. They were, at best, only moderately well informed about scientific parapsychology. They were not associated with any occultist groups of the sort that, as Stevenson (1984) put it, "thrive on the fringes of parapsychology" (12). Typically, C. J. used his knowledge of hypnosis to help friends and parishioners.

As for the content of her principal communications in German, Gretchen said that her name was Gretchen Gottlieb and that she lived with her father in Eberswalde, Germany. Her father, Herman Gottlieb, was the mayor of that town. He was rather old and had white hair. Her mother, Erika, had died when Gretchen was about eight years old. She had no brothers or sisters. Occasionally, she mentioned a grandparent, but more frequently referred to Frau Schilder who did the household cooking and seems to have been employed as a housekeeper. Frau Schilder did not live with the Gottliebs. She came during the day, bringing several of her own children. Gretchen said she lived on Birkenstrasse; and she said that Eberswalde was a small town, with a river not far away and a forest nearby. The town had a college, a church, a butcher shop, and a bakery. Stevenson goes on to characterize further the content of Gretchen's story:

> Gretchen could tell little about her daily life. She appears to have passed most of her time in the kitchen playing with Frau Schilder's children, and regarded

herself as to some extent assisting in their care. [The youngest of these children was, she said, only three years old.] She could describe rather well the food she ate. She did not go to school and had never done so. She explained this by saying that young girls did not attend school. She said that she could not read or write. Sometimes Gretchen referred to herself diffidently as being "stupid" [in German "*dumm*"]. She seemed uninformed about the geography and current politics of the period in which she lived. She could not name any large city near Eberswalde, although Berlin, the capital of Prussia and later of the German Empire, is approximately 45 kilometers southwest of Eberswalde. She said that Darmstadt, which is more than 400 kilometers away was "near." She was, on the other hand, quite definite that the head of the church was the Pope, and when asked his name, she said it was Leo. Concerning her knowledge of Martin Luther, Gretchen made different statements at different times . . . almost always, however, she spoke of Luther adversely as a troublemaker and the person responsible for the strife in her neighborhood of which she claimed to be a witness . . . Gretchen rarely spoke spontaneously; usually she remained silent until asked a question. She would then reply briefly and fall silent again. Her manner was always polite and a little deferential, like that of a well-behaved child. On several occasions, however, she rather firmly corrected some mispronunciations by C. J. of a German word or set straight an interviewer who misheard what she had said. (Stevenson 1984, 15)

Gretchen spoke frequently of the trouble between the church and the government but she intimated that it was not a good idea to talk about it. She seemed fearful of being watched by the *Bundesrat* (a town governing council/town government).

From various things Gretchen said, incidentally, Stevenson was able to piece together, roughly, the time (the 1870s) and the general area of Gretchen's life. But owing to the difficulty of determining the precise location of Eberswalde, and to other difficulties with regard to the content of Gretchen's story, the existence of this Gretchen Gottlieb has not been verified, and so, unlike in other cases such as the Bishen Chand Case, any connection between the Gretchen personality, and an actual person of past times has not yet been established.

As in the Lydia Johnson (*qua* Jensen) case, the knowledge that the Gretchen personality manifested regarding her own historical time and place is precisely what one would minimally expect of a person living there and then. Moreover, in both cases the argument is that—even when we cannot verify the actual historical existence of Jensen and Gretchen—we have no way to explain the linguistic skills and the other knowledge that the subjects have unless we appeal to reincarnation as the most plausible hypothesis. We will touch on this again later when we examine specific objections to the Gretchen Case as evidence for reincarnation.

Let us now turn to the last of the language cases under consideration here.

MEMORY EVIDENCE AND RECOGNITION: THE SWARNLATA CASE

In 1951, an Indian man named Sri M. L. Mishra took his three-year-old daughter Swarnlata and several other people on a 170 mile trip, south from the city of Panna (in the district of Madhya Pradesh) to the city of Jabalpur, also in the same district (see Stevenson 1978, 78ff). On the return journey, they passed through the city of Katni (fifty-seven miles north of Jabalpur), Swarnlata unexpectedly asked the driver to turn down a certain road to "my house." The driver quite understandably ignored her request.

Later when the same group was taking tea at Katni, Swarnlata told them that they could get better tea at "my house" nearby. These statements puzzled her father, Mishra; neither he nor any member of his family had ever lived near Katni. His puzzlement deepened when he learned that Swarnlata was telling other children in the family further details of what she claimed was a previous life in Katni as a member of a family named Pathak. In the next two years, Swarnlata frequently performed for her mother, and later in front of others, unusual dances and songs that, as far as her parents knew, there had been no opportunity for her to learn. In 1958, when she was ten years old, Swarnlata met a woman from the area of Katni whom Swarnlata claimed to have known in her earlier life. It was at this time that Mishra had first sought to confirm the numerous statements his daughter made about her "previous life."

In March 1959, H. N. Banerjee began to investigate the case, and in 1961 after Banerjee's investigation, Ian Stevenson went to Chhatarpur to recheck carefully the work done by Banerjee. From the Mishra home in Chhatarpur, Banarjee had traveled to Katni where he became acquainted with the Pathak family of which Swarnlata claimed to have been a member. He noted before journeying to Katni, some nine detailed statements Swarnlata had made about the Pathak residence. These statements he confirmed upon his arrival. Incidentally before Banerjee went to Katni, the Mishra family did not know or know of the Pathak family.

Banerjee also found that the statements made by Swarnlata fit closely to the life of Biya, a daughter in the Pathak family and the deceased wife of a man named Pandy who lived in Maihar. Biya had died in 1939—nine years before the birth of Swarnlata.

In the summer of 1959, members of the Pathak family and of Biya's marital family traveled to Chhatarpur, where the Mishra family lived. Without being introduced to these people, Swarnlata recognized them all, calling them by name and related personal incidents and events in their various lives with Biya—events that, according to these relatives, only Biya could have known. For example, Swarnlata had known that, as Biya, she had gold fillings in her front teeth. Biya's sister-in-law confirmed as much. The Pathaks eventually accepted Swarnlata as Biya reincarnated, even though they had never previously believed in the possibility of reincarnation. After these visits, in the same summer, Swarnlata and members of her family, went to Katni and then to Maihar where the deceased Biya had spent much of her married life and where she died. In Maihar, Swarnlata recognized additional people and places, and commented on various changes that had occurred since the death of Biya. Her statements were independently verified. Later Swarnlata continued to visit Biya's brother and children, for whom she showed the warmest affection. The songs and dances that Swarnlata had performed presented some problems, however. Biya spoke Hindi and did not know how to speak Bengali, whereas the songs that Swarnlata had sung [and danced to] were in Bengali.

Although the songs were publicly available and had been recorded on phonograph records and played on certain films, she could not have learned these songs from records or films because her parents had neither seen nor heard them and, therefore, Swarnlata, as a typical child under close surveillance of her family—had no occasion to do so. The parents were also certain that Swarnlata had not been in contact with Bengali speaking persons from whom she might have learned the songs. Swarnlata claimed that she had learned the songs and the dances from a previous life. Stevenson noted that this was a case of recitative, rather than responsive, Xenoglossy because she could not have conversed in Bengali although she could sing Bengali songs (Stevenson 1974, 14).

After careful reflection and examination, Stevenson concluded that it is very difficult to explain the facts of the case without admitting that Swarnlata had paranormal knowledge (PK). After all, how otherwise could Swarnlata have known the details of the family and of the house? These details (including the fact that Biya had gold fillings in her front teeth—a fact that even her brothers had forgotten) were by no means in the public domain. Moreover, how otherwise can we explain her recognition of members of the Pathak and the Pandey families? How can her knowledge of the former (as opposed to the present) appearances of places and of people be explained? Her witnessed recognition of people amounted to twenty in number. As Stevenson noted, most of her recognitions occurred in such a way that Swarnlata was obliged to give a name or state a relationship between Biya and the person in question. On several occasions, serious attempts were made to mislead her or to deny that she made the correct answers, but such attempts failed.

Could there have been a conspiracy among all the witnesses in various families (the Mishras, the Pathaks, the Pandys)? Might not all of them have conspired to bring off a great hoax? Well, according to Stevenson, a family of prominence such as the Pathaks, with far-reaching business interests, is unlikely to participate in a hoax involving so many people, any one of which might later defect. If a hoax did occur, it is more likely to have come from the Chhatarpur side. But even here Sri M. L. Mishra had nothing to gain from such a hoax. He even doubted for a long time the authenticity and truth of his daughter's statements, and he made no move to verify them in six years. Most of the people involved agreed that they had nothing to gain but public ridicule.

But even if we suppose there was some attempt at fraud, who would have tutored Swarnlata for success in such recognitions? Who would have taken the time to do it? Sri M. L. Mishra, apart from Swarnlata, was the only member of the family who received any public attention from Swarnlata's case. And what attention he received, he was not happy about. Also, how could M. L. Mishra get some of the highly personal information possessed by Swarnlata about the private affairs of the Pathaks (for example, that Biya's husband took her 1,200 rupees)?

Might Swarnlata have been tutored by some stranger who knew Katni and the Pathaks? As Stevenson noted, like all children in India—especially girls—Swarnlata's movements were very carefully controlled by her family. She never saw strangers in the house alone, and she never was out on the street unaccompanied (Stevenson 1974, 14).

Besides the legal documentation and methods used in Stevenson's examination, what is interesting about this case is that it is one of many similar cases. Can we explain the facts plausibly without appealing to the belief in reincarnation? Before we explain such facts let us examine our last case study.

THE CASE OF THE THIRD JAMES

James Leininger, son of Andrea and Bruce Leininger of Lafayette, Louisiana, was a problem when he was two years old. His parents reported that he began having terrible nightmares about a plane crash. By the time he was three years old, he informed his parents that before he was born, he was a pilot who flew from a boat until his plane was shot in the engine by the Japanese, causing him to crash into the water and that is how he died. People wondered if he was remembering the life of an actual pilot.

There was an ABC television interview of the parents and the boy. For various reasons, however, it was not aired. Two years later, another interview was filmed by ABC. This newer interview was aired. By this time James' parents had been able to verify much of what James had said even as his story had become more extraordinary.

James now said, for example, that he had been a pilot named James on the boat *Natoma* and that he had been shot down at Iwo Jima. He also reported having had a friend named Jack Larsen. James' father discovered that a James Houston from the USS *Natoma Bay* had been shot down in the two Iwo Jima operations, and another pilot on the USS *Natoma Bay* was a fellow named Jack Larsen.

Shortly thereafter, Dr. James "Jim" B. Tucker, who is an Endowed Research Professor of Psychiatry and Neurobehavioral Sciences in the Medical School at the UVA, and who is currently the Director of the UVA Division of Perceptual Studies, secured friendly permission from the parents, Bruce and Andrea, to study this case and research it closely in Louisiana. Initially, however, they wanted to delay any interviews with James until they had finished publishing their own book on James's story. Tucker and his colleagues actively continue with the work and research of Ian Stevenson, on children and others who report memories of previous lives.

Incidentally, Tucker had explained to James' parents how potentially important their story could be because it was an American case, and one in which a complete stranger who had been killed sixty years ago was positively identified as the previous person the child claimed to be. The case was quite possibly unprecedented for various other reasons. But it took six years before Tucker could sit down to discuss the experiences of the Leininger family—Andrea, Bruce, and James.

By this time, James was about to turn twelve years old. Most children who claim to remember a past life, usually stop talking about their memories by the time they are six or seven years old. So, when Tucker got down to interviewing the family and seeking to verify the most salient facts, he was not particularly optimistic. Even if James was still talking about his past life, he might now have heard much about James Huston, and if, as Tucker (2013) in *Return to Life* noted, "he did not show a knowledge of specific items he had not had the opportunity to acquire normally, his statements would provide little evidence that he was in fact remembering a past life" (66). In any event, he forged ahead.

Tucker's primary research interest was in what young James had said before anybody identified James Huston as the pilot whose life James was remembering as his own. He began by interviewing Bruce, James's father, in the Leininger's dining room in Louisiana, while James and Andrea went elsewhere. Bruce had kept some research records of what James said from the beginning in a small bookcase.

According to Bruce and Andrea, the first incident in their story occurred when James was twenty-two months old. At the time, the family was living in

Texas and Bruce took him to the Cavanaugh Flight Museum in Dallas. Before that, James would point at planes that flew overhead, but at the Museum he became transfixed. He kept wanting to return to the World War II exhibit. He and Bruce ended up spending three hours at the Museum because James was so fascinated by those planes, and they left with a few toy planes and a video on the Blue Angels, the U.S. Navy's flight exhibition team.

When James played with the toy airplanes, he repeatedly crashed them into the family's coffee table saying, "Airplane crash on fire." Also whenever Andrea and James took Bruce to the airport for a business trip, James would tell him: "Daddy, airplane crash on fire."

James' nightmares began a couple of months after the visit to the Museum. Andrea would find James thrashing around and kicking his legs up in the air, screaming "Airplane crash on Fire! Little Man can't get out!" (Tucker 2013, 69). This nightmare occurred regularly night after night. Visiting often, Andrea's sister often saw them and described them as watching somebody terrified and fighting for his life. They included blood-curdling shrieks from James, as he kicked his legs toward the ceiling, screaming about an airplane crash and a big fire and proclaiming, "Little Man can't get out!" (69).

Several months into the nightmares, one night when Andrea was reading James a bedtime story, He said, "Little Man is going like this" and re-enacted his dreams, kicking his legs up in the air and saying "Can't get out" (Tucker 2013, 69). Until this night, Bruce thought that the nightmares were a typical childhood event. But this was his son talking about these things when he was wide awake. Bruce asked him what happened to his plane. James said it crashed on fire. Bruce asked him why and James said it was because it was shot. And Bruce asked him who shot the plane and James said "The Japanese!" (69). At this time, James was a little more than two years old.

A couple of weeks later, Andrea and Bruce had another bedtime talk with James who said his plane was a Corsair, a fighter plane developed during World War II. He talked on several occasions about flying a Corsair, and skeptics noted that the Cavanaugh Flight Museum has a Corsair on display. So, James might well have seen the Corsair when his father took him to the Museum. Skeptics inferred that James probably saw the plane there and the name stuck in his mind. In response to that allegation, Bruce told Tucker that in his research there was no Corsair in the Museum when Bruce and James visited. There had been one, but it had crashed in an air show and was only replaced later. Tucker looked into the matter and found out that Bruce was correct. A Corsair that was on loan from a Museum had crashed at an air show in Wisconsin on July 29, 1999, six months before Bruce had taken James to the Cavanaugh Museum for the first time. Tucker called the Cavanaugh Flight Museum about the Corsair they have now. The woman working at the Museum told him that the current one was a replacement for the one that had crashed in 1999, and that the Museum obtained it around 2003. James did not see one on his trip to the Museum and at twenty-eight months of age, he must have known the name from somewhere else (Tucker 2013, 69).

Along with saying that night that he flew a Corsair, James also said he had flown off a boat. When Bruce asked him if he remembered the name of the boat, James said "*Natoma.*" Bruce replied that "*Natoma*" sounded Japanese. James said no, that it was American.

Later, Bruce searched online for information on the word *Natoma*. He found a description of USS *Natoma Bay*, an escort carrier stationed in the Pacific in World War II. Bruce printed out the information and kept it so we have a second copy of it. Each page of the printout has the name of the website as the footer, along with the date the pages were printed "08/27/2000." In this way we know that Bruce was searching for *Natoma* when James was twenty-eight months old.

Tucker further noted that some of the specifics of this case were dependent on the accuracy of Bruce and Andreas' memories; but not this. Tucker notes that unless we think this is an elaborate fraud, with this Christian couple in Louisiana faking a case of past life memories despite potential derision by friends and neighbors, we need to conclude that little James did give the name *Natoma* (Tucker 2013, 69).

When Bruce and Andrea would ask James who the little man in the plane was, he would say "me" or "James." A month or so later, he came up with another name. When his parents asked if there was anyone else present in the dream with James, he gave the name Jack. They asked if he had another name and he replied "Jack Larsen" (Tucker 2013, 74).

The Leiningers asked James, "Was Jack James' friend?" James replied, "He was a pilot too" (Tucker 2013, 74). James' father, Bruce, decided he would conduct a search for one Jack Larsen. He searched the World War II database on the American Battle Monuments Commission website on 10/16/2000. Bruce gave a copy of the search on that date to Tucker who repeated it. It shows one Jack Larsen, one John Larsen, one Jack Larson (spelled with an o), and four John Larsons. That site only includes those who are buried on the Commission's cemeteries or who are listed on the walls of the missing. It only lists casualties. The Jack Larsen from the USS *Natoma Bay*, as it turned out, had survived the war.

Tucker conducted his own search for Jack Larsen. He went to the registry on the National World War II Memorial Site. It combines four databases, though the one with survivors is unofficial and incomplete. Tucker found nine listings for men who served in the U.S. Navy during World War II. He found that ships did not typically have a "Jack Larsen" on board. But *Natoma*, the ship James had named, had a Jack Larsen on board. Bruce had not searched for a living person; he assumed that if James' dream was in fact a memory, it was about being Jack Larsen. Bruce basically thought that James was reporting a dream about somebody named Jack Larsen. Bruce's wife, Andrea, however, was not so focused on Jack Larsen because, as she said, she had asked James thirty times what his name was in the dream, and he always said James. He said Jack Larsen was a friend with whom he flew.

About a month after mentioning Jack Larsen, James was just over two and a half years old, and Bruce ordered a book, *The Battle for Iwo Jima 1945*, for a Christmas gift. He was looking through it one Saturday morning when James climbed into his lap. They opened to a place that showed a map of Iwo Jima on one page. On the other page, there is a photograph from an aerial view of the base of the island, where Mount Suribachi sits. According to Bruce, James pointed to the picture and said, "That's where my plane was shot down." When Bruce asked him "What?" James answered "My airplane got shot down there, Daddy" (Tucker 2013, 88).

A week later Bruce had his first talk with a USS *Natoma Bay* veteran. He had found a reference to the *Natoma Bay* Association online and called one of the contact numbers. The man he talked with had served on the *Natoma Bay* during the Iwo Jima operation. He remembered a pilot from the ship named Jack Larsen, but he did not know what happened to him. He said Larsen flew off one day and they never saw him again. Bruce assumed that what that meant was that Larsen did not return from a flight and became missing. At that point Bruce had solid confirmation that there was a ship named *Natoma Bay*, that it was at Iwo Jima, and that Jack Larsen had been a pilot on it. At that point, as Tucker tells us, some puzzle pieces were still missing. In the meantime, Andrea took up the practice of talking to James about his nightmares immediately after he had them, and they reduced in frequency and in intensity. James also began talking more about his nightmare memories when he was awake.

Soon after his third birthday, James began drawing pictures of battle scenes with ships and planes over and over again. His parents said he drew hundreds of them. He began to sign the pictures "James 3." When his parents asked him why he did that he said, "I'm the third James. I'm James 3." Tucker checked on this with both parents and they both agreed that he said, "I am the third James." They have drawings he made after he turned four that still say "James 3" on them. What it may refer to is that James Huston was a junior. As Tucker notes, that would make James Leininger the third James (Tucker 2013, 88).[6]

When James was three and a half years old, he talked about his plane getting shot. Bruce asked him where it had been hit. James pointed to the front of the engine and said the plane had been hit right in the propeller. It had one-propeller mounted on the nose of the plane.

In September 2002, when James was about four and a half years old, Bruce went to his first USS *Natoma Bay* reunion. He told the veterans that he was writing a book about the ship. During the reunion he learned that although Jack Larsen was not at the reunion, he was still alive. He had not gone missing. He had merely left the *Natoma Bay* for another assignment. Bruce had also learned that only one pilot from *Natoma Bay* had been killed during the Iwo Jima operation, a twenty-one-year-old soldier from Pennsylvania named James Huston. In 2004, when Bruce's interview took place, Bruce quoted that James was saying "That's when my plane got shot" (Tucker 2013, 88). And not *where*. James Houston's plane was shot down in the Iwo Jima operation, but not actually over Iwo Jima itself.

The pilots of USS *Natoma Bay* made 123 flights in the Iwo Jima operation in the days before the start of the invasion and another on February 19, 1945, when the assault began. When the Japanese were preparing an increase in troop replacement, pilots from the *Natoma Bay* took part in a strike against transport vessels in a harbor on Chichi-jima, which was about 165 miles from Iwo Jima.

The aircraft action report filed after the event notes the following: "Heavy anti-aircraft put the planes under fire from both sides of the harbor. James Huston's plane was apparently hit by the fire as the plane approached the harbor entrance" (Tucker 2013, 88). None of the other pilots saw that his plane was hit, but it suddenly careened into a forty-five-degree glide and crashed into the water. It exploded and burned, and by the time two of the other pilots could get to the area, no wreckage of the plane was still afloat. This happened on March 3, 1945, four days before the USS *Natoma Bay* completed its work in the Iwo Jima operation.

According to Tucker's research, there was no way to confirm that James' plane had been shot in the engine. The aircraft action report from Huston's squadron stated that none of the ship's other pilots had seen his plane hit.

The *Natoma Bay* crew was not the only source of information, however. Bruce posted a query about Houston's crash on the website about Chichi-jima. A month later, he received a call from a veteran from another ship who had witnessed Houston's plane get hit. He had flown off the USS *Sergeant Bay*, which had also taken part in the attack. His plane had also been hit that day on its second run. On its first one, he had seen a fighter from *Natoma Bay* "take a direct hit on the nose" as he had written in an informal memoir (Tucker 2013, 76).

Bruce talked to three other men who had seen Houston's plane get hit, and they all told the same story. One of them said Houston's plane was very close to his, and that he and Houston actually made eye contact just before Houston's plane was shot in the engine and quickly engulfed by flames. Another veteran had been interviewed on the ABC *Primetime* segment, and he said "I saw the hit. I would say he was hit head-on, yeah, right on the middle of the engine" (Tucker 2013, 77).

James also said that Jack Larsen was there when his plane crashed. The aircraft action report for the day Houston was shot down includes a drawing of the paths each pilot took; Larsen's plane was next to Houston's.

All this data matched what James had said before his parents began researching James' story when he was two and a half years old. Andrea said in an interview before all this data was found, that one day James told her: "Mama, before I was born, I was a pilot, and my airplane got shot in the engine and it crashed into the water, and that's how I died." Andrea also said in that segment that James had said that his plane took off from a boat and that it was shot down by the Japanese (Tucker 2013, 77).

By way of offering a brief conclusion, this carefully documented research leads to the poignant and inescapable conclusion that James, as early as two and a half years old, had the confirmed personal memories of James Huston's death, and that young James identified himself reliably with James Huston, when James Huston had died a hero's death many years before little James was born. The salient point here seems to be that, owing to the excellent research conducted professionally by James' parents, and to Tucker's focused confirmation of the parents' research, Little James had the personal memories of James Huston, and explicitly claimed that he was James Huston.

How could anybody have the empirically confirmed personal memories that only the deceased could have had without being that person? And how could little James be James Huston without being the confirmed reincarnation of James Huston?

THE ARGUMENT STATED: WHAT BETTER EXPLANATION?

The six case studies above exemplify in varying degrees, the ideal typical characteristics of the Six Core Features (1 through 6) mentioned above in conjunction with Stevenson's (1978) generalized argument. Of course, in the Bishen Chand case, the interviews were not taped, but they were written down. In general, most of the interviews were taped whenever possible. And Swarnlata did not speak in an unlearned foreign language, or like Bishen Chand, play an instrument she had not learned to play; but she did sing in a foreign language that she had not been taught, and she did perform complicated dances that she had never seen.

Both subjects provided memory information about facts that were not in the public domain, and yet were subsequently verified by independent investigators. Also the accuracy of their memory claims down to the smallest detail was much too high to be explained in terms of PSI (ESP) or probability, or blind luck, or coincidence. The large number of extant family members who provided extensive verification of the memory claims about personal and very private historical details is particularly important. Not only because of the methods employed in examining these cases, but also because of their richness of detail, arguably these cases collectively typify the strongest sort of evidence for personal reincarnation.

The Mrs. Smith case may not match all Stevenson's (1978) ideal typical characteristics in his Six Core Features, involving as it does a long ago past life. But the recitative Xenoglossy exhibited by Mrs. Smith, and her consistent memory of previously unknown but later often verified historical facts, qualify the case as worthy of serious consideration in the context of this study.

Further, the Lydia Johnson (*qua* Jensen) case, and the D. J. (*qua* Gretchen) case also do not contain all the Stevenson ideal characteristics of 1 through 6 stated above. But they were taped extensively in the presence of Stevenson's colleagues. We still have no success in explaining these subjects' capacity to speak in an unlearned language and to describe successfully so many of the historical details of the past lives they depict without appealing to reincarnation. Or so it would seem.

At this point then, the argument for minimalist personal reincarnation is very simple. It is this. What would be a better or even more plausible explanation for these cases than to assume that some human personalities have in the past reincarnated?

Opponents of belief in reincarnation will need to provide an equally plausible or better alternative explanation for the data in these and other cases if they are to successfully undermine the claim that the best available explanation for the data is belief in personal reincarnation. On that point we can now turn to some of the more prominent candidates for alternative explanations that do not require belief in personal reincarnation. There are several such proposals. Owing to limitations here on space we will concentrate only on what seem to be the most challenging.

BYPASSING ESP, THE SKEPTIC'S RESPONSE

In an essay titled "Are 'Past-Life' Regressions Evidence of Reincarnation?" Melvin Harris (1986) argued that all reincarnation-type cases in which people are regressed and describe details of past lives are actually fascinating instances of *Cryptomnesia*. He believes that we can explain memories of past lives by saying that in all cases the information the subjects convey about past events has been acquired quite normally from sources such as parents, newspapers, lectures, radio, TV, books, and so forth. Shortly after acquiring the information, the subjects forget it. And when under hypnotic regression, they later remember what they normally learned, they have forgotten the origin of information. Because they have forgotten its origin, they naturally identify the information as the product of memories of those events.

In reply to this objection, we should note that Harris (and others) tends to generalize from one or two cases to all cases in which regression is used. Moreover, anybody who actually reads Stevenson's (1974; 1975; 1978; 1980; 1984; 2001) work will readily see that he includes no cases that could be explained by appeal to *cryptomnesia*.

Similarly, who could have taught Lydia Johnson eighteenth-century Swedish, or Gretchen, a regional non-standard German? Indeed, one of the criteria for a rich case—a criterion Stevenson explicitly states from the beginning—is that we not be able to explain it by appeal to cryptomnesia, and in every case he offers reasons why cryptomnesia does not work as an alternative explanation. In every rich case, there are facts to which the subject has testified that are subsequently confirmed but that nobody alive could have known.

GENETIC MEMORY?

A second alternative explanation asserts that we need only suppose that everybody is born with a certain genetic memory—that just as we inherit the genetic physical traits of our ancestors so too the memories of our ancestors are coded in our genes. Then, so the argument goes, under certain circumstances the inhibitors of these traits are relaxed, and the memories of our ancestors emerge. When these memories come, they are experienced by the subject as though they were the subject's own memories.

In this alternative explanation, we are asked to believe that Bishen Chand, for example, inherited Laxmi Narain's memory (even the memory of how to play the drums and to speak Urdu) and mistakenly identified these memories as his own. Similarly, Lydia Johnson inherited the memories of Jensen Jacoby, and this extends to remembering how to speak Jensen's language. In both cases the subjects obviously mistakenly believed that what they were remembering were events in their own respective lives. In fact, they were remembering events in the lives of others who had passed those memories onto their ancestors in and through the gene pool. Is this explanation any more forceful than that based on cryptomnesia?

Not really. If the appeal to the phenomenon of genetic memory were the proper explanation for Bishen's knowledge of Laxmi Narain's life, then we would expect Bishen to be in Laxmi Narain's genetic line—though clearly he was not. This point was emphasized by Stevenson, and it seemed to be the most important factor in many Xenoglossy cases that strongly suggest reincarnation (Stevenson 1974, 342). That is, no genetic connection is discernible between the subject and the alleged ancestor whose language the subject can speak. In the case of Lydia Johnson and Jensen Jacoby, tracing the genetic line is pretty much out of the question.

But as the explanation of genetic memory does not apply in many of the richer cases described above, it seems that the appeal in general will not work. In some of the strongest cases, we know for certain that no genetic line connects the subject to the allegedly reincarnated person.

Besides, as Stevenson (1980) has also argued, this explanation will not work in those cases where the subjects describe in rich detail the manner of their own death: "A parent could only transmit genetically to his or her offspring memories of parents that had happened to the parent before that child's conception. It follows therefore that the memory of the person's mode of death could never be inherited" (359). This seems to be a conclusive reason for rejecting the argument that past life memories are simply inherited from one's ancestor through natural genetic mechanisms. Additionally, it does not explain the more interesting cases. Finally, what also undermines the skeptic's appeal to genetic memory is the fact that, while some purely genetic traits (such as the genetic diseases Huntington's Chorea, hemophilia, and Phenylketonuria, or PKU) are non-dispositional, other genetic traits are dispositional. That is, we inherit the disposition—more or less—to certain traits. Quite clearly the emergence of the actual trait requires some input from the environment.

The acquisition of a skill such as speaking a language cannot be explained in terms of an inherited trait, because contemporary genetics tells us to view the ability to speak a language as a function of an inherited ability plus an additional component supplied by the environment. And, this holds equally well for the ability to play an instrument.

LINGUISTIC POSSIBILITY?

The linguistic objection urges that a closer look at the regression cases in which subjects allegedly speak an unlearned language appropriate to a particular past life reveals that the subjects are so lacking in fluency that we cannot reliably say that they know the language they are said to speak without having learned it. Sarah Thomason (1987) offered this objection in her article "Past Tongues Remembered?" Thomason's claim is that, if we scrutinize carefully the Gretchen case, we will see that of 172 possible responses made by Gretchen in German to questions asked in German, only twenty-eight answers are appropriate, and that we surely do not need a paranormal explanation of her knowledge of so few German phrases. Even a limited exposure to German books, or to World War II movies, could explain whatever fluency is present (for my reply see Almeder 1988; and her answer in Thomason 1988).

To this objection we can offer three basic replies. First, Thomason (1987) illegitimately generalizes from one case. Second, her objection overlooks the force of the fact that we would all say a man knows how to speak German if, when asked questions in German, he responded in German appropriately to twenty-eight of them. We still need to explain how somebody who was never taught to speak German can successfully understand that language enough to respond successfully to unrehearsed questions twenty-eight times. Third, we cannot plausibly explain the latter by appeal to World War II movies or casual glances at German books. In such movies or books, one would need to understand what was being said. Besides, this latter explanation would never work in the Lydia Johnson (*qua* Jensen) case where the subject is responsively reasonably fluent in eighteenth-century Swedish. We cannot explain successfully Jensen's limited but appropriate responses by appeal to casual contact with books, movies, or people speaking Swedish. There are other deficiencies involved in Thomason's (1987) analysis, such as the criteria employed for what counts as an appropriate answer, but these three replies should be sufficient to make the point. Let us now turn to other objections and explanations, and to the general charge of fraud and hoax.

PARAMNESIA?

The fourth alternative theoretical explanation is the appeal to *Paramnesia*. This objection asserts that the so-called favorable evidence for reincarnation can be easily explained and dismissed by taking certain cultural facts into consideration. In this explanation, the young child makes a few statements that, in a culture strongly disposed to belief in reincarnation, the gullible parents interpret as memories of a past life. They then proceed to encourage the child to make more statements, and frequently ask leading questions. From the material they so derive from the child, they identify a deceased person whose life fits, more or less, with the statements. The parents then rush to the family of the deceased to relate what the child has said. The latter family, still grief stricken over the deceased member, accepts uncritically the statements as corresponding to the life of that member. The child is asked to answer more questions and is frequently asked to identify family members with patently obvious cues and leading questions. The families exchange information about the child's memories. Thereafter, informants on both sides credit the child with more detailed memories than they had. There is no conscious fraud or hoax in all of this; it is simply the result of cultural conditioning combined with sloppy methodology. The fact that most of the evidence garnered in most cases has come from spontaneous past life memories, the contents of which are typically conveyed to researchers by members of the families involved—and that little of it has been induced by investigators in direct interviews with the subjects—makes this a reasonably persuasive objection. In fact, some critics regard it as the most decisive refutation of the allegedly most compelling cases.

Stevenson (2001), for example, takes paramnesis quite seriously. In his *Children Who Remember Previous Lives*, he grants that this objection certainly applies in a certain number of cases—those wherein the families involved have contact with each other before researchers can take testimony from the subject (if possible) and from the family members (150–53). And Stevenson (1975) has published reports on such cases wherein this objection turns out to be the decisive reason why those cases cannot be taken seriously. For this reason also, Stevenson (1975; 1980; 2001) has published reports on cases wherein the families apparently contacted each other before independent researchers were summoned, and hence cannot be regarded as clearly acceptable evidence.

Paramnesia breaks down for more than a few cases. Among other reasons, it certainly would not apply in more than twenty very rich cases in which someone made a written record of what the child said before there was any verification of their statements (Stevenson 2001, 150–53). Nor would such an explanation fit the Xenoglossy cases described above (Stevenson 1974).

SLOPPY METHODOLOGY?

Apart from paramnesia, but related to it, there is a general methodological objection often heard. According to this objection, we should be more skeptical about these so-called typical case studies of personal reincarnation, primarily because the investigators typically show up on the scene quite some time after the child initially makes the memory claims, and they then depend on the parents' or relatives' memories and interpretation of what the child in fact said and did.

Then again, altogether too often some of these allegedly compelling cases require the services of a language translator, and this introduces an even deeper possibility for misunderstanding just what the principals are asserting. Given these possibilities of error, there is just too much room for honest mistakes in describing and verifying the salient features of the presumptively richer case studies. As this objection goes, until we can minimize the significant potential for error associated with the methodology, it is unscientific to accept the case descriptions at face value, as indicative of actually what happened. Hence, even if we can eliminate all possibilities of fraud and of deception in the richer cases, the data are too problematic to take seriously as proper evidence.

To the general *sloppy methodology* objection, we can offer two replies. The first is that the same objection applies to most historical knowledge and to eyewitness testimony to past events. Thus in itself, the objection is not enough to discount the data—not until one can positively show that the testimony is mistaken, or more likely than not mistaken, in the case at hand. The second reply is that more often than not, the richer cases are rich precisely because the probability of this sort of error is quite remote. Often no translation is involved; the time gap between the origination of the case and the investigation is not significant; and the number and variety of independent witnesses provide a check for the accuracy of crucial testimony. We need only look closely at the recent cases described above to see that this objection is implausible, given the actual details of the cases, and the careful way in which they were investigated.[7]

TWO MORE SKEPTICAL RESPONSES

We should acknowledge two more basic and common objections. The first is that the *minimalist reincarnation hypothesis* is not scientifically established because the data and the results are not repeatable by independent researchers using the same careful methodology. This first objection is also unacceptable for two reasons. First, the thesis is empirically reproduced each and every time a non-fraudulent case, such as the case of Bishen Chand, emerges. That we cannot produce the cases at will is no more probative against reincarnation than is our inability to produce more dinosaur bones at will counts against the verification of past existence of dinosaurs.

Belief in the past existence of dinosaurs is both empirically verifiable and verified as the best available explanation of the cause for the data consisting of certain footprints and other skeletal remains. Similarly, belief in the past existence of Julius Caesar is simply the best available explanation for certain historical data. Doubtless, it is possible that Julius Caesar never existed and that somebody falsified certain public records in some way or other. But in the absence of solid evidence that the possibility of error in these instances is no more than a mere logical possibility, we do not have any empirical grounds for questioning our beliefs in the past existence of dinosaurs or of Julius Caesar. What makes these two beliefs empirical or scientific is not that we can produce *at will* robustly confirming data for these beliefs, but rather that we know what evidence it *would take* to either falsify or verify our hypotheses.

Similarly, we know what it takes to verify or to disconfirm the belief in personal reincarnation. More cases like that of Bishen Chand, for example, will continue to verify the hypothesis; and unquestionable evidence of fraud or of hoax will falsify the hypothesis. But even though the logic of the situation is the same with respect to reincarnation, we are skeptical about belief in reincarnation as an empirically confirmed belief.

The difference lay in the fact that belief in reincarnation commits us to the present existence of an object that is not, in principle, directly observable by the methods currently available in natural science, whereas belief in the past existence of dinosaurs or Julius Caesar does not so commit us.

Nevertheless, as this is the reason for the difference, we should note that belief in the existence of theoretical component of say, quarks, muons, or psions, accounts for certain data, but nobody can observe such entities. Belief in such entities is simply the best available explanation providing reliable predictions of our sensory experiences based on the data.

The second reason to the first objection is that it is just not true to say that the minimalist reincarnation hypothesis is not an empirically confirmed thesis for the alleged reasons that the evidence and the result are not repeatable. The evidence *is* obviously repeatable in principle, but it is certainly not reproducible at will. Sometimes, for example, we will need to wait patiently for confirming evidence provided by nature unpredictably.

The second skeptical response in this section is the long-standing *population objection*. It notes that the human population has increased dramatically from 8000 BC when the global population was roughly 5 million, to the present 6 billion, and the world's population will be approximately 8 billion by the year 2021. From this math, it is supposed to follow that the thesis on reincarnation is false. But why exactly?

The evidence for past reincarnations does not imply that a set number of persons will continue indefinitely to reincarnate. Nor does the evidence show that new persons are not created, just as it does not imply that the process of reincarnation is eternal. Certainly, there is nothing logically impossible here. Is it then that the thesis of reincarnation requires that at any given time there will be more persons waiting in line for bodies than there are reincarnated persons? Well, if it did, so what? This is not a reason for thinking that belief in reincarnation is false, but could, rather be seen as an implication of the thesis itself. The data for reincarnation *per se* do not preclude special creation, the creation of new persons with new bodies. Nor does the data entail it, or require it. There is no factual evidence currently explaining the increase in reincarnated persons. But, reincarnationists do not need to explain as much, because *the evidence for reincarnation would establish the thesis* no matter what the best explanation may be for an increase in reincarnated persons, if there were an increase in the number of reincarnated persons.

To summarize, taking seriously the population objection requires making assumptions about the number of persons there are, the duration of the process of reincarnation, and the uncreated (that is, the newly uncreated) and limited number of persons. None of these assumptions is necessary. Nor are they implied by the data for personal reincarnation. The most that we can say is that if personal reincarnation has occurred in the past, then the number of reincarnated persons *may* have increased along with that population—unless of course not everybody reincarnates sooner or later, and that new persons are often created. In short, the population objection appears irrelevant to the question of the truth of the belief in personal reincarnation.

THE PENELHUM OBJECTION

Many philosophers and scientists still urge that personal reincarnation is impossible because bodily continuity is a necessary condition for having personal memories. According to this view, it makes no sense whatever to suggest that memory, or a systematic set of personal memories, could survive biological death. For them, personal identity will require personal bodily continuity as a necessary condition for personal identity.

Terrence Penelhum's (1970) argument for this view begins by asserting that a person can remember something only if their memory claim is true. He then goes on to say why no account of disembodied identity can be given:

> This requires that we should be able to distinguish between those occasions when what someone thinks he remembers actually happened to him, and those occasions when they did not. This we cannot do in terms of the recollections themselves. There has to be some independent way of determining that the person who did or experienced what Smith believes he remembers doing or experiencing was, or was not, Smith himself. And this, it seems, has to be his physical presence at the occasion in question. (Penelhum 1970, 70; see also S. Shoemaker 1970).

There are at least two persuasive responses to Penelhum's (1970) argument. First of all, we can surely infer from the nature of the recollections themselves that this person (Smith) *was physically there*, because there is no other way to account for them knowing what in fact took place before they died when there is no public record of that event, and when *nobody except somebody who was there could possibly know about it*.

For example, if Smith claims to remember having hidden his blue pocket knife in a certain precise location in 1648, and if we can ascertain that nobody else now knows (or ever knew) where the pocket knife was hidden, and there is demonstrably no public or private record of the event, then we are certainly at liberty, *upon finding the blue knife where Smith says it is*, to conclude that Smith remembers where the knife was hidden—even if we determine that the knife was hidden in 1648 when he secretly hid it.

Similarly, there are several personal memories that only Napoleon could have had; and if somebody claims to remember some events that *only* Napoleon could have remembered, the belief in reincarnation explains how he could have this information, and experience it as a genuine memory or personal recollection.

Second, as we noted earlier, Penelhum's (1970) argument begs the question. After all, granting that in order to determine whether a man, say, remembers (rather than falsely claims to remember) something or other, we must establish that he was at the event allegedly remembered—who is to say that when determining whether *he* was at the event allegedly remembered, the personal pronoun *he* must refer to his present body rather than to the one he previously occupied? Is this not precisely the question at issue?

Is this not, for example, exactly what the data from cases suggestive of reincarnation question? Is not the reincarnationist, who bases their belief on the sort of data provided by Stevenson and others, trying to explain the baffling fact that some people seem to remember events they could not possibly have personally witnessed so long as we construe personal identity in terms of bodily continuity? If the only response we can offer is that they do not in fact remember what they claim to remember because it is impossible that one could remember anything before one was born into one's present life, then the reincarnationist wants to know precisely why we should adopt an a priori conception that would render personal reincarnation (as well as discarnate survival generally) conceptually impossible when, in all other respects, *the hypothesis of reincarnation fits an important body of data not otherwise currently capable of explanation.*

The reincarnationist, then, will recommend that we hesitate to assume an interpretation of the nature of memory that makes reincarnation and discarnate personal survival conceptually impossible, rather than look at the data and see whether it might make sense to understand the definition of memory in a way that is at least neutral to the question of personal reincarnation.

Openness to the empirical data allows us to infer that memory and personal identity are not tied to bodily continuity. It may also lead us to believe that so and so must have been present at the physical event he claims to remember because there is currently no other way for us to explain the demonstrable accuracy and richness of what he claims to remember.

But obviously they could not have been there in their current body. Why should we not regard the belief in personal reincarnation as an inference to the best available explanation of the empirical facts in the richer cases offered by Stevenson and several of his colleague researchers around the globe?

As such, it would be a justified rejection of any conception of memory under which one can only remember those events one witnesses in one's current lifetime as a biological organism. Ultimately, then, our second reason for rejecting Penelhum's (1970) argument is that it begs the question against belief in reincarnation.

PERPLEXING QUESTIONS

At this point, unavoidable and perplexing questions will emerge. To begin with, what about the stranger we left back on the park bench, and who claimed to remember having lived as Julius Caesar? Should we say that the stranger making the claim *is* Julius Caesar? Again, as we argued above, if he has some memories that only Julius Caesar could have had, and if we actually confirmed robustly those memory claims, then we ought to accept that this fellow is Julius Caesar reincarnated, and then try to live with the mystery of how and why that can happen.

In the Bishen Chand case, for example, the subject seems to have an identity and memories that Laxmi Narain could not have had—unless the subject simply *is* Laxmi Narain in a new body with a new name. If so, we would expect the subject in such cases to identify themselves accordingly. We would expect them to say something such as "I am Laxmi Narain here to continue my former existence." Such locutions occur. Sometimes we also hear that subjects say "I used to live in such and such a place, and I did such and such."

But we also hear other expressions—expressions that seem to imply that the subject is not Laxmi Narain, for instance, but remembers having lived as Laxmi Narain without now being Laxmi Narain.

So, is it Laxmi Narain remembering that he lived an earlier life and is now continuing that life with additional memories derived from his current life in a new body designated by the name Bishen Chand? Or is it another person, Bishen Chand, part of whose personality contains the personality of the former Laxmi Narain? Would Bishen Chand's memories of this life, in other words, be simply Laxmi Narain continuing in a new body (which has picked up a new name) and *adding or fusing more clear memories to the memories of Laxmi Narain*? It seems very natural to explain the phenomena here in this latter way. But might it not also be that Bishen Chand is a distinctly different person who has subsumed, as part of his own identity, the person Laxmi Narain was? It seems equally natural to describe the phenomenon this way. *But it cannot be both.*

In the end, for any number of reasons we might simply *need to decide* which way to describe it, and it is unclear at the moment whether we can decide by appeal to the facts alone in the cases already examined. Even if we asked the people in these cases, it is very possible that their answers would be philosophically slanted or the product of antecedent bias. But perhaps we ourselves can use a philosophical approach to determine which way to describe it.

Suppose then, for the sake of discussion, that the second way of describing the phenomenon is correct, that is, that the person, Laxmi Narain, exists simply as a subset of the personality of Bishen Chand, or is subsumed or blended somehow into the identity of Bishen Chand. Is there any separate person to be identified with the name Bishen Chand? Is Bishen Chand one person rather than the collection of two persons blended or fused under one name? Is the person Bishen Chand simply a composite of both Laxmi Narain and whatever other person is to be identified with the memories that are not the memories of Laxmi Narain.? If only to have an adequate story about human personality, it seems important to answer this question. But can this question be answered non-arbitrarily?

Hard to say. On the one hand, all we can discern at this point is that the problem *per se* seems to emerge as a result of endorsing the second description.

Suppose, on the other hand, that for the sake of discussion, the first way of describing the phenomenon is correct, that is, that Bishen Chand is actually Laxmi Narain continuing on happily in a new body and adding more memories and dispositions to his existing personality. Given this first description, when we ask Bishen Chand "Who are you?" and he responds "Bishen Chand" what has he told us? Has he told us who he is? Certainly not—because we want to know who the person Bishen Chand *really is*. The name "Bishen Chand" simply designates a body some person occupies—a person evolving through various connecting reincarnations, and therefore continuously in transit, as it were.

Moreover, we will not know who Bishen Chand really is until we get beyond asking "And who is he?" or "And who is she?" When we get back to the original person who began this reincarnation process, however, we now have a problem. Is that person really the person Bishen Chand is? Hardly. The person who Bishen Chand is now cannot be identified with the person who started the process, namely, Laxmi Narain. The body of memories that Bishen Chand now has are dramatically different from the memories of the original person. But if this is so, how can we ever identify who anybody *is*?

Although these problems may have less to do with the strength of the evidence for personal reincarnation than they have to do with the logic of personal identity, special sorts of problems will surface depending on just what we mean when we say, "So and so is the reincarnation of so and so." The evidence supports one of the above descriptions and not both, but one of them may be more philosophically congenial than the other on the grounds that accepting one of the descriptions may lead to a peculiar kind of absurdity (such as "nobody knows who anybody is") or to a theory of human personality that could not in fact be true.

There are other pertinent questions here. Consider the following.

If you reincarnate will you be pretty much the same person in your next body as you are now? Yes and no. If you have essentially the same traits and memories in the next body, yes. If you add dramatically to those traits and memories because of being in that body, no. But if the latter occurs, will the person you now are disappear? Yes, in the same way something may evolve into something it now very much is not. One's personality would not so much disappear from the earth as it would evolve into something very much unlike what it formerly was—owing to the activities and the chemistry experienced in the new body.

However, this is not to suggest that some people do not survive death as persons; for we often become persons very different from the persons we were. *Still, something essential to us must remain throughout the process.* Unfortunately, it is difficult to say what this something is.

Indubitably, if it is difficult to say what this something is, how can one be so sure of what we should take as evidence that the man or the lady beside us on the bench is the reincarnation of Julius Caesar? Intuitively we do not seem to have any problem with this, because most philosophers agree at least on memory as the criterion of personal identity.[8]

> Even so, questions about personal identity remain; and though we may fail in our efforts to say clearly what human personality is, our core intuitions about what counts for identifying distinct personalities are sufficient to sustain the belief that some human personalities in some important measure survived biological death, in some way, and to some degree reincarnated. Whether the reincarnated person is just the former person with a new body creating new memories, or whether the reincarnated person is in some way a distinct personality that has subsumed into itself the former person without losing its own identity, or whether the reincarnated person is a blended or a composite of some sort as suggested above—*is still problematic.*

However we decide, it will be on the basis that minimal reincarnation has in some way occurred in the past, even though we do not know how it happened, how it was caused, why it was caused, how long it will go on, and what the point of it all may be.

SCIENTIFIC POSTSCRIPT: REINCARNATION AND THE PROBLEM OF PERSONAL IDENTITY

Arguing the case for personal reincarnation, even in minimalist terms, requires a considerably more nuanced discussion of other objections than we can pursue here. Even so, we can reflect briefly on some wider implications and perplexities of confirming empirically that some people have indeed reincarnated.

As I argued in the last chapter, if a stranger claimed to be Julius Caesar reincarnated, we would be free to accept his claim if, and only if, he had some of the personal memories we would ordinarily expect Julius Caesar to have had, along with some personal memories that *only* Julius Caesar could have had. Moreover, if the stranger conveyed these memories in fluent Caesarian Latin, or played well the ancient instrument we know Caesar played; and if we could establish that the stranger had never learned Caesarian Latin or how to play this ancient instrument without learning how to do so, we would have credible evidence that this man really is Julius Caesar reincarnated. Again, of course, these personal memory claims would need to be independently verified—especially the personal memories that *only* Caesar could have had.

However, a refusal to accept this stranger's verified memory claims and acquired skills (not learned in this life) as persuasive evidence for belief in reincarnation seems like a dogmatic refusal to accept any and all evidence for belief in personal reincarnation. Again, how can we explain the stranger's knowing what only Julius Caesar could have known, without believing that he is Julius Caesar?

Many philosophers may insist that while personal identity is a matter of having a certain set of systemic and independently verifiable memories, including memories of events the subject has personally witnessed, personal discarnate survival (and by implication reincarnation) is quite impossible because bodily continuity is necessary for having personal memories. According to this view, it makes no sense to suggest that memory, or a systematic set of personal memories, could survive bodily corruption. After all, mental events, as they say, supervene on physical properties in some way or other. If they are right, the wages of presumptive materialism and physicalism will need to be shown, rather than to be assumed.

As we also saw above, Penelhum's (1970) argument began by asserting that a person remembers something only if their memory claim is true. Penelhum then ventured to say why no account of disembodied identity can be given. He said, as we may recall:

> This requires that we should be able to distinguish between those occasions when what someone thinks he remembers actually happened to him, and those

occasions when they did not. This we cannot do in terms of the recollections themselves. There has to be some independent way of determining that the person who did or experienced what Smith believes he remembers doing or experiencing was, or was not, Smith himself. And this, it seems, has to be his physical presence at the occasion in question. (Penelhum 1970, 56)

We also noted above, the two possible replies to Penelhum's argument. First, we can surely infer from the nature of the recollections themselves that this person was there, because there may be no other way to account for their knowing what in fact took place when there is no public record of that event and when nobody except somebody who was there could possibly know about it.

Second, we suggested that Penelhum's argument is also question begging. After all, granting that in order to determine whether a man, say, remembers (rather than falsely claims to remember) something or other, we must establish that he was at the event allegedly remembered—who is to say that when determining whether "he" was at the event professedly remembered, the personal pronoun "he" must refer to his present body rather than to the one he previously occupied? Is this not precisely the question at issue? Is this not, for example, what the data from cases suggestive of reincarnation question?

Is not the reincarnationist who bases their belief on the sort of data provided by Stevenson and other colleagues, trying to find an explanation for the apparently baffling fact that some people remember events they could not possibly have witnessed so long as we construe personal identity in terms of bodily continuity? If the only response we can offer is that they do not in fact remember what they claim to remember because it is impossible that one could remember anything before one was born into one's present life, then the reincarnationist seeks to know exactly why we should adopt an a priori definition of memory. Such a definition would make personal reincarnation conceptually impossible, *when in all other respects the hypothesis of reincarnation fits an important body of data not otherwise capable of explanation.* In the end, then, our second reason for rejecting Penelhum's (1970) argument was that it begs the question against reincarnation in particular.

NOTES

1. In his book *The Problem of Knowledge*, A. J. Ayer (1956) saw nothing contradictory about the *possibility* of personal reincarnation. He said that if Julius Caesar's personal memories about personal events known only to Julius Cesar were revealed by a living human in great detail and were subsequently shown to be true, then Ayer initially confessed that he would not know what to say. But he granted that the living

person claiming to be Julius Caesar might *really* be Julius Caesar. He thought that that conclusion was a rational decision, but he *preferred* to think that the fellow claiming to be Caesar also might have had some mysterious powers of being able to access Caesar's memories without being Caesar. So, in the end, Ayer affirmed that the question of reincarnation calls for a decision that might be most useful and not a matter of fact (193–96). In short, he waffled.

In any event, Ayer was steadfastly committed to bodily continuity as the primary criterion for personal identity and that therefore it seemed impossible to him that we should end up with the concept of a "person" extending to some non-physical substance, not unlike a Cartesian immaterial substance.

2. The major objection to any memory theory of personal identity was offered briefly by Reid (1785/1969), and later at greater length by Williams (1957). The objection consists in a thought experiment in which a fellow named Charles turns up claiming to be Guy Fawkes, described in chap. 1. As I see it, however, this counterexample fails. If Robert did show up satisfying the memory criteria for being Guy Fawkes, that would be an empirical disproof of the memory theory of personal identity. as an instance of definition by way of appeal to ordinary usage, rather than an empirically falsifiable thesis

3. The justification of this idealizing condition lay in the fact that its satisfaction would diminish the force of the objection that the subject subconsciously identifies and impersonates the deceased person's traits clairvoyantly grasped. For further discussion on the rationale behind this condition see Stevenson (1978, 169ff and 359–60).

4. See Stevenson (1978, 145ff). Here again, this idealizing condition has for its purpose to distinguish between the psychiatric phenomenon identified with multiple personality or alternating personality and with cases of reincarnation in which the subject claims to be an extension of the previous personality.

5. Incidentally, Stevenson (1984) claimed that Gretchen introduced no fewer than 237 words, 120 of them spoken in ten sessions before anybody spoke German to her (33); and he offers a list of well-formed German phrases of expressions spoken before anybody spoke German to her (37).

6. Tucker (2013) notes that Andrea's sister told him the following story that Bruce and Andrea had not told him. One day Bruce slapped a map of the world down on the table and he asked James "Okay, where is Little Man's plane?" James pointed in the Pacific Ocean, and the adults leaned down and saw that his finger was on a group of islands called the Ogasawara Archipelago. There in microscopic writing was the name Iwo Jima. Bruce confirmed the story and sent to Tucker copy of the map. Spread across two pages and measuring twenty-two inches by seventeen inches altogether, Tucker notes that it is remarkable that a three or four-year old could identify any specific place on it "much less the location where events he was describing from a past life took place" (74).

7. Owing to editorial constraints on space here, I will postpone a fuller discussion of other objections and replies to the minimalist belief in personal reincarnation. In particular, I would examine more fully the most recent and the most common objections, such as the "Reincarnation cannot be empirically verified because we do not

know how it happens or what the cause is," the LAP or Super-Psi alternative explanation that I still find non-falsifiable. For a fuller treatment of other objections and possible competing explanations of the data in the richer of the cases, I recommend, however, Almeder 1996a, 495–533; and Almeder 1992. Also, I reviewed negatively Paul Edwards' (2011) *Reincarnation* (see Almeder 1988).

8. I hesitate to enter into the commanding literature on personal identity and the criterion of personal identity. However, I warmly recommend Kim and Sosa 1999, part 2, for a compelling group of essays on the related issues.

Chapter 3

Objections and Replies to the Minimalist View of Personal Reincarnation

INTRODUCTION: OBJECTIONS AND REPLIES

This chapter offers additional objections to the minimalist view of Personal Reincarnation as described and defended previously. These objections, criticisms, and evaluations were published, in part, over the years in different journals and in collections by other researchers seeking to provide sound alternative scientific explanations in an effort to reject the data and other arguments offered as far back as 1990 through 2015.

Next, you will find discussions published in 1996 in the *Journal of Scientific Exploration*, volume 10, issue 4, and in the journal *Philosophia* between me and other philosophers and scientists who are interested in some major arguments flowing from earlier exchanges in *Philosophia* and elsewhere (Almeder 1996a; 1996b; 2001; Hales 2001a; 2001b). The nuanced replies focused on alternative examinations of the data provided by critics of reincarnation case studies.

Some of the items examined in the first two chapters are here described in more detail and in the light of other recent discussions on "The ET Hypothesis" and on how deeply the reincarnation data provided here needs to be embedded in current and well-confirmed scientific theories.

THE ET HYPOTHESIS

The first objection we revisit here is philosophical and called the "The ET Hypothesis." Its author, Steven Hales (2001a), provided an alternative anti-survivalist explanation for personal reincarnation data in the *more recent* cases examined above (344).

The second objection also appears in a critical review and in my response to other arguments flowing from earlier discussions and objections of the empirical data in the richer cases. Unlike the ET Hypothesis however, the second objection appears in earlier publications including *Death and Personal Survival: The Evidence for Life After Death*, but arguably it requires more clarifying discussion (Almeder 1992).

The third objection also offers an anti-survivalist explanation of the data in the richer reincarnation case studies. That explanation is that this murky paranormal world is more likely to be some form of fraud, deception, or clever deceit than are the alleged cases of minimal personal reincarnation as described previously.

HALES' HYPOTHESIS

According to Hales (2001a; 2001b), then, we can find the best set of arguments for personal survival and personal reincarnation in the book *Death and Personal Survival* (Almeder 1992). He also rejects the argument that it would be *irrational* not to believe in some form of personal reincarnation after examining the relevant data proposed in the best-case studies. Hales finds that argument striking. However, he does not believe it.

PARFIT'S JAPANESE WARRIOR

Hales also revisits Derek Parfit's (1984) argument to the effect that we might have had strong empirical evidence for personal reincarnation if, for example, we had come across a Japanese woman claiming to remember living her life as a Celtic hunter and warrior in the Bronze Age. On the basis of her *apparent* memories she might make many predictions that could be checked by archeologists. Thus she might, for example, claim to remember having a bronze bracelet, shaped like two fighting dragons. "And she might even claim that she remembers burying that bracelet at a certain location beside some particular megalith, just before the battle in which she was killed. Archeologists might now find just such a bracelet buried in this spot, and their instruments might show conclusively that the earth had not been disturbed for 2000 years. The Japanese woman might make many other predictions, all of which are verified" (227).

So, Parfit's argument, as we noted several pages ago, added two more conditions to the effect (a) that there is no physical continuity between the Celtic warrior and the Japanese woman, and (b) that we must discover many cases much like this one. Hales (2001a; 2001b) also adds that Parfit believes that in fact we have no such evidence of this sort in order to justify belief in personal reincarnation (Parfit, 1984, 228).

As we also saw previously in passing, A. J. Ayer (1956) at one time argued that if he came across several cases similar to Parfit's Japanese woman, and if we could not then find a plausible alternative explanation of the data, he could justifiably conclude that the person before him is indeed reincarnated.

However, Ayer (1956) later changed his mind on what to conclude on this story (193–94).

In criticizing my position, incidentally, Hales (2001a) agrees, along with others, that the assertion "It is irrational or epistemically irresponsible not to believe in reincarnation given the current empirical evidence" is false (346). His justification here rests in his belief that the best of reincarnation case studies are not embedded in well-accepted theories in natural science. More on this below.

FLEW'S REJECTION OF REINCARNATION EVIDENCE

Hales' argument further echoes Antony Flew's (1956) claim that the evidence for personal reincarnation is not repeatable under scientifically controlled experiments. For Flew there are no reincarnation laboratory experiments . . . and so he claims that the evidence for personal reincarnation is *anecdotal* at best, and could never aspire to provide scientifically acceptable confirming data. Therefore, concludes Hales (2001a; 2001b), we are never scientifically justified in believing that some persons have indeed reincarnated.

Elsewhere, the examination of Flew's claim that the evidence for reincarnation could never aspire to furnish reliable scientific evidence for reincarnation for lack of acceptable experimental data, and hence is once again merely anecdotal.

A CRUCIAL DISANALOGY

In response to the above objections we all surely know, for example, that dinosaurs existed possibly millions of years ago. But the data confirming the past existence of dinosaurs was not the product of any scientific experimentation similar to laboratory experiments. Previously undiscovered dinosaur bones cannot be produced at will under lab conditions. Nor can we produce at will human subjects that satisfy the demands of excellent case studies confirming that some people have personally reincarnated (Almeder 1992, 55–57).

At this point Hales (2001a; 2001b) asserts that the evidence for personal reincarnation is crucially *disanalogous* to the evidence for the past existence of dinosaurs. The past existence of dinosaurs is consistent with our best empirical theories about the world, whereas reincarnation is not consistent with either the best of our empirical theories or with our best philosophical theories about the mind.

Hales (2001a; 2001b) then alleges that most contemporary philosophers regard the best theory about the mind to be some basic version of reductive materialism. Hence the analogy to the belief in the past existence of dinosaurs is weak on the face of it. He further adds that nobody offers even a sketch of a theory that would be able to account for all of the current data about the mind, while also explaining how, by what mechanism, human personality could survive death and reincarnate.

Hales (2001a) *further affirms* that the case studies favoring reincarnation and depicted in chapter 2, amount to blindly venerating data over theory (339). He notes that raw outlier data of the sort provided by reincarnation case studies lack evidence for any scientific theory, and thus offer no explanation of the *how* and the *why* personal reincarnation occurred.

RESPONDING TO HALES

In brief response to Hales' (2001a; 2001b) comments, we saw above and in various places that there is no demonstrable evidence that confirms reductive materialism, or the view that the only objects in this world are physical objects governed by the Laws of Physics under Natural Selection.

Second, again, the strong reincarnation cases show only *that*, and *not how* or *why*, some people have reincarnated because the case studies offer the best available story on how the current empirical data was provided in the best cases to date. *Our conclusion is admittedly and joyfully inconsistent with reductive materialism.*

But then again reductive materialism is *demonstrably not a scientific theory*. Rather, it is a gratuitous commitment or assumption, however useful it may be in predicting human events and behavior. Hales (2001a) asserts, unfortunately, that reductive materialism is warmly accepted among most well-established scientific theories (342).

Finally, Hales (2001a) applauds the ET Hypothesis, which he describes as an alternative competing hypothesis superior to the personal reincarnation hypothesis. He asks us to *assume* that there are intelligent, technologically advanced *Extra-terrestrials* who find humans amusing, and secretly monitor and sometimes interfere with our lives. They enjoy, for example, performing super-advanced psychosurgery on select humans that provides these humans with *quasi-memories* of having lived past lives, verifiably true beliefs about where ancient bracelets are hidden, and previously non-existent linguistic or musical skills. He adds that, unlike a Cartesian evil genius, the ET Hypothesis is perfectly testable by empirical means if these aliens were to land and reveal themselves and their techniques, this would serve to confirm the hypothesis (342). If, however, we were to completely survey the universe and find no such superior Extra-terrestrials this would *falsify*, or *undermine*, belief in such creatures.

Hales (2001a) claims that this ET Hypothesis is perfectly *consistent with materialism about the mind*, and it explains the cases as well as the personal reincarnation hypothesis (342).

In fact, Hales thinks that the ET Hypothesis and the Reincarnation Hypothesis are equally plausible hypotheses. Each consistently fits the data equally well. So, on the basis of the data we would have no more justification for accepting one hypothesis than the other.

When all is said and done, the ET Hypothesis depicts a state of affairs that is certainly imaginable and logically possible. But what are its empirical test conditions? How would we confirm this hypothesis? Hales (2001a) says that we do not know how empirically to confirm this hypothesis. Along with Parfit (1984), he believes that *we have no current valid empirical evidence favoring belief that anybody has ever reincarnated.*

However, we do know how to confirm the *Reincarnation Hypothesis*. We only need to know what its test conditions are. In other words, we only need to find somebody who claims to remember, for example, being Cleopatra and who can provide us with many personal confirmed memories that *only* Cleopatra could have had. She might even tell us that on the day before she died, she secretly buried a farewell note to Antony and buried it at a certain location ten feet deep and known only to Antony. But she died before telling him where the note was buried. No scientist or researcher has ever found that note at the designated location. Now, we only need to test the veracity of her personal memory by finding and exhuming the note with Cleopatra's farewell signature. If we find it where she remembers the note was buried, we have confirming evidence that the person before us is in fact Cleopatra reincarnated. If she has several more similar personal memories we can empirically confirm in the same way, then we have empirically confirmed that the person before us is indeed Cleopatra reincarnated. Again, we may not *know* how this happens, or even *why* it happens. Nor does this singular confirmation show that everybody reincarnates. In conclusion, the ET Hypothesis *is not demonstrably and empirically testable, whereas we do know how to test empirically the Reincarnation Hypothesis.*

VACUOUS REDUCTIVE MATERIALISM

Some Question Begging

It is also Hales' (2001a; 2001b) view that the data in case studies of the sort described previously by Ian Stevenson (1974; 1975; 1978; 1980; 1984; 2001) and his colleagues does not count alone to confirm belief in personal reincarnation, primarily because, as he argues, the data must be embedded in or consistent with well-established scientific theories.

But, as Hales affirms, since the majority of scientists strongly accept some form of reductive materialism, any body of data from case studies affirming belief in reincarnation, would be inconsistent with well-established scientific theories. In other words, the data from case studies cannot confirm belief in reincarnation because reincarnation is logically inconsistent with well-established widely adopted physical theories on minds and on consciousness.

And yet, as we frequently noted, belief in any form of reductive materialism, however widely adopted by members of the scientific community, remains an assumption or a commitment without confirmation. So, logical inconsistency of reincarnation data supporting personal reincarnation is certainly inconsistent with widely adopted forms of reductive materialism, but it does not need to be embedded in any wider theory that starts with the assumption favoring some version of reductive materialism.

Appealing to reductive materialism of any sort as a necessary condition for justifying the belief that some people have reincarnated seems to be question begging at the very least.

THE INCONSISTENCY BETWEEN PERSONAL REINCARNATION AND REDUCTIVE MATERIALISM

At the risk of repetition, there is indeed a demonstrable inconsistency between *Reductive Materialism* and the belief in *Cartesian Immaterial Substance*. Let us return to a second alternative explanation of the data, namely, the explanation that appeals to Psi or Super-Psi.

THE PSI AND SUPER PSI HYPOTHESIS: ONE MORE TIME

The Braude Arguments

In *Death and Personal Survival* and elsewhere, I have examined the *Psi-Hypothesis*, or explanation, for data that would otherwise strongly support some form of personal post-mortem survival (Almeder 1992, 42–47, 51–53, 117–120, 151–154,195, 264). But this Psi-Hypothesis is tenacious. And so I shall revisit it and then advance the effort to show that reincarnation and survival data are not well explained by appeal to Psi or to Super-Psi. In fact, the Psi-Hypothesis as a possible alternative hypothesis to explain the data in survival cases is an instance of René Descartes' (1985) evil demon hypothesis, and is an appeal to a totally *ad hoc* and untestable (hence unverifiable and untestable) hypothesis. In contrast, however, the reincarnations as well as the personal survival hypothesis are considerably more plausible because they are quite empirically testable and straightforwardly falsifiable.

Stephen Braude (1986; 1989; 1992a), along with the late Jule Eisenbud and others, have argued, elsewhere, that an equally plausible explanation for data in reincarnation cases, for example, may well be that the subjects in these cases are not reincarnations, but rather they are people who have these very special paranormal abilities allowing them to replicate the propositional and non-propositional skills that otherwise seem to support belief in reincarnation. On this view, for example, Bishen Shand's memories of his alleged earlier life as Laxmi Narain, including the memories that only Narain could have had, could well be attributable to ESP, or at least it is not implausible to think that need-based Psi is the cause of the data here and in similar cases. So on this view, it is not implausible to think that Bishen, through some form of ESP, was able to acquire the memories of Laxmi Narain, and then mistakenly believed, for purely psychological reasons based on deep need of some sort, that he was in fact Laxmi Narain. And Bishen's ability to impersonate Laxmi Narain, even though he had never seen him, is also plausibly construed as a paranormal ability activated by strong needs-based desire or stress.

Similarly, in those rare cases of active Xenoglossy, wherein the subject has not only the memories of a certain past person but also the non-propositional skills (such as speaking in a foreign language the subject has not learned and which the person who has allegedly reincarnated spoke fluently), the possible explanation offered by Braude (1992a) for the subject having this propositional and non-propositional knowledge that it is equally plausibly a function of ESP or Psi. He sometimes calls it "Super Psi" (as opposed to "puny psi" or "dandy psi") and refers to it as ESP, or paranormal knowledge (PK), on a grand scale. Thus for Braude (1992a) we can plausibly justifiably explain all the data in these richer cases as simply a product of a form of PK which, however interesting, is ultimately only an emergent and irregular property of brains under unusual circumstances (127–44).

Braude also believes that a careful psychological examination of such subjects is as likely to show an important explanatory and causally possible connection between the subject's ability to generate such data and deep psychological motives not always obvious to either the subject or the investigators.

Independently of Braude's (1989; 1992a) claim that we know Super-Psi exists even though we cannot produce it at will in laboratory settings, one of Braude's reasons for taking Super-Psi as seriously as a possible, or equally plausible, alternative explanation for data in rich reincarnation, is that any denial of such a claim is in fact a matter of placing arbitrary limits on the extent and the magnitude of Psi when in fact we do not know enough about Psi to justify such an imposition and how it works. Braude says:

> Given our present state of ignorance concerning the nature of psi, we must, at the very least entertain the possibility of extensive psi. . . .
>
> In fact, the only way we could ever be entitled to exist that psi effects have inherent limits would be on the basis of a thoroughly developed and well-supported full scale psi theory, one that embraces the totality of available evidence for psi [not just no. 2 laboratory evidence], and explains why or how psi functions both in and out of the lab. But at present no decent theory forbids large scale or super-psi, and certainly no scientific study [most simply ignore it], and certainly no scientific study renders any form of psi improbable. (Braude 1992a, 127–44)

Braude (1989; 1992a) also contends that arguments dismissive of Super-Psi as a possible alternative explanation of so-called survival evidence are *severely defective*. On this issue, he engages the following three standing objections to the existence of Super-Psi: (1) There is no evidence for the existence of super-psi; (2) There is evidence against super-psi; and (3) The super-psi hypothesis is not falsifiable.

In response to the first of these objections, Braude (1989) claims that it assumes we would know Super-Psi if we saw it, and that this assumption is the first objection clearly indefensible because there need be no observable difference between a heart-attack or a plane crash caused normally and one caused by PK (or Super-Psi). The only difference may be in their unobservable causal histories (29). He claims further that those who assert the first objection are also guilty of the more general methodological mistake of offering only theory-dependent arguments, that is of using arguments and data that presuppose the denial of super-psi (33).

In response to the second objection, Braude (1989) argues that, contrary to what some have asserted, we know of no established limits of super-psi and that large scale super-psi might occur surreptitiously in less contrived, or ritualized human circumstances outside the lab (33).

Finally, in response to the third objection, Braude (1989) admits that the existence of super-psi is not falsifiable, but he is quick to add that non-falsifiability is theoretically uninteresting and certainly does not undermine the super-psi hypothesis.

In response to the super-psi hypothesis, I agreed in *Death and Personal Survival* that there is empirical evidence for the existence of Super-Psi or Psi on a grand scale, and that it may function in ways distinct from our current understanding of what the limits of ESP and of PK may be (Almeder 1992, 52ff). That, of course is the striking point of Braude's (1986) *The Limits of Influence: Psychokinesis and the Philosophy of Science*.

Furthermore, doubtless nobody should place any a priori limits on what forms Psi may take in the future. That said, however, there is something very dissatisfying about offering Psi, or some form of Psi, as a plausible possible alternative explanation for the data in the richer survival cases, including reincarnation cases.

The main problem seems to be that, as Braude (1986; 1989; 1992a) and others describe it, the existence of Super-Psi, or sneaky Psi, as a causal agent in these cases is neither confirmable (because, as he says, we cannot empirically distinguish it from normal physical causes) nor falsifiable. Insisting that we should empirically confirm the existence of Psi, or sneaky Psi, as a particular causal agent in some way before appealing to its existence to explain anything in particular, is less a matter of erroneously assuming *a-priori* limitations on Psi or PK than it is simply a request for some evidence of the causes cited in the proffered explanation. If a possible alternative explanation is not in any way empirically testable, as indeed it would not be if it could not be falsified or confirmed, there is no way the explanation could have any apparent empirical validity. There would be no apparent way to discriminate empirically between an explanation offered in terms of Psi and one offered in terms of usual causal agencies in the world. We cannot know that Jones is the robber of the Rabun Gap Bank if we cannot distinguish between Jones and Brown who might equally well have robbed the Bank.

Moreover, if no empirical evidence, (that is, public sensory evidence implied by the truth or falsity of hypothesis could ever count either for or against Jones' robbing the bank, and if the supposition that Jones is the robber has no other testable implications), we might just as well claim that an angel robbed the bank on a whim, or that God did it. Its total lack of testability, in terms of some distinctly empirical data that would allow us to adjudicate between it and any competing alternative hypothesis, is what renders the

Psi hypothesis a pseudo-hypothesis (see Hempel 1966, 33). Carl G. Hempel (1966) says:

> But if a statement or set of statements is not testable at least in principle, in other words, if it has no test implications at all, then it cannot be significantly proposed or entertained as a scientific hypothesis or theory, for no conceivable empirical finding can then accord or conflict with it. In this case, it has no bearing whatever on empirical phenomena, or as we will also say, it lacks empirical import. (Hempel 1966, 30)

Similarly, if nothing empirical could count for the existence or non-existence Super-Psi, the hypothesis appealing to it as an explanation or the data in the richer survival cases seems empirically meaningless. Some form of empirical testability, and by implication falsifiability or confirmability, is simply a necessary condition for any hypothesis being an empirically significant hypothesis. Here again, if we do not know what to accept for the falsity of a hypothesis (such as sneaky psi being at work), then anything and everything could count as positive confirming instance of the hypothesis; and this makes the hypothesis meaningless because it is vacuously confirmed. Appealing to so-called higher order criteria (such as explanatory fecundity, simplicity, and systematicity) for theory selection seems quite pointless if the meaning of the hypothesis cannot be clearly specified in terms of the evidence that would need to be present for justifiably rejecting or accepting the hypothesis.

Braude is (1989) dismissive of falsifiability as a necessary condition for empirical significance because, as he says:

> It is foolish and arrogant to think that the only phenomena or hypotheses worth discussing are those that conform to our preferred forms of empirical investigation . . . such an attitude is the adoption of an "old fashioned rigidly Popperian Stance" because we can justifiably reject an explanatory hypothesis (for pragmatic reasons) even when it is not conclusively falsified. (Braude 1989)

In response to Braude's reasons for disparaging falsifiability as a necessary condition for the plausibility of any empirical explanation, we might note that it is neither arrogant nor foolish to insist upon falsifiability as a necessary condition for empirical significance, because without it we have no way of determining whether the hypothesis is true or is false. If the hypothesis makes no specific predictions at the sensory level that tend to support the hypothesis, or tend to undermine it, then nothing at the sensory level could count either for or against the hypothesis; and the Psi hypothesis makes no specific predictions at the sensory level, least of all that it should ever appear again in this world. That is why the Psi hypothesis is not falsifiable as an empirical hypothesis about data in survival cases.

Along with Rudolf Carnap (1936), some of us continue to believe that a primary end of cognitive inquiry is the production of some predictions of our sensory experience, which only falsifiable explanations can provide. Hypotheses that serve that purpose provide us with adaptive power, generally, and nature will select out whatever methods provide for such predictions as a reliable, belief-making method for understanding the physical world.

Nor is the adoption of "Falsifiability," as a necessary condition for a legitimate explanation of physical phenomena, the adoption of an "old-fashioned rigidly Popperian stance." It is simply the insistence that if an hypothesis is to count as a potential explanation for physical phenomena it must have some test implication by way of providing deductively specific predictions of sensory experience expected if the hypothesis is true or if it is false. How one goes about testing the hypothesis is indeed an interesting, and when exactly the hypothesis has merited robust acceptance in terms of the various kinds of tests conducted is also an interesting question (see Braude 1989, 9).

But what is not an interesting question is whether empirical hypotheses need to be tested and confirmed or falsified in terms of their deductive implications at the sensory level. Otherwise, acceptance or rejection of theories or hypotheses is made on a purely arbitrary basis and provides no reasonable grounds for expecting anything at the sensory level as a result of such an acceptance or rejection. This is standard empirical practice, and if the hypothesis is not testable, and hence not falsifiable, in terms of what the hypothesis predicts of sensory phenomena, then nobody in the scientific community would regard it seriously because if it is not falsifiable, then it is vacuously confirmed even if it provides no specific predictions. We do not rationally reject an empirical hypothesis when it is not falsified in terms of test conditions of the hypothesis in question.

Moreover, it is certainly not the case that the acceptance or rejection of empirical hypotheses depends, as a rule, on *higher level* pragmatic considerations that have nothing to do with whether hypotheses are empirically testable (and hence either falsifiable or confirmable in terms of the test implications of the hypotheses at the sensory level). If two hypotheses are equally well-confirmed by the data, then we may be at liberty to choose one over the other until such time there is provided a better or more precise set of predictions of sensory phenomena. But just because various testable and falsifiable hypotheses equally fit the data or the evidence as possible hypotheses, does not imply that we decide on one over the other on purely pragmatic grounds.

If the appeal to Psi is meant to offer a plausible alternative explanation of the data, it is not offering a scientific explanation. And if there is some other way of explaining empirical phenomena, we need to know what will count as a successful explanation in that area. How would we distinguish between a good and a bad explanation when falsifiability and confirmability, in terms of sensory implications, are not at issue? Appealing to the so-called Pragmatic Considerations of a higher order is consistent with willful belief, regardless of what the facts may be. Otherwise, as an hypothesis in science, appeal to Psi as a possible plausible alternative would not seem to be any better than the famous hypothesis of neo-vitalism in biology; it predicted (and retrodicted) nothing specific that would count for its confirmation or falsification, told us nothing about how it affected biological organisms, when and how it begins to work, and led to no fruitful expectations.

This is not to say that one may not have private knowledge of the existence of Psi or Super-Psi. Private knowledge, incidentally, is the knowledge one would have if it is based on evidence that is quite transitory, non-repeatable, and hence, accessible only to the subject for a limited amount of time. But "Private Knowledge" is, by definition, not the public knowledge we seek in natural science, and there is no reason for anybody to accept an item of private knowledge as an item of public knowledge. Moreover, even if we could show empirically (as Braude has, I believe) that Psi, Super-Psi, or sneaky Psi has existed in the past, it still would not follow that appeal of any form of Super-Psi is a plausible explanation of the data in the better survival cases because we would not know what would count for falsifying the hypothesis (see Braude 1989, 35). Claiming, as Braude (1989) does, that the fact that the Super-Psi hypothesis is not falsifiable, is of no theoretical consequence, or is of little theoretical interest, seems false and is very revealing, because if the thesis is not falsifiable, then once again it is difficult to see how any appeal to Psi as a causal explanation can be anything other than vacuously true (because in principle non-falsifiable) *a-priori true*, and evidence of a dogma.

Of course, if Super-Psi can be so sneaky, its presence undetectable and unpredictable, one can only wonder how Braude (1989) succeeded in establishing that it ever existed in any past circumstances. The perplexing point here is that he did apparently succeed, in my view, because the hypothesis was the best then, and now, given the above reasons we need to have some independently available reasons to explain the empirical data in question (11).

But this conclusion of itself affords no independent plausibility at all to the view that such forces are at work, accounting for the strongest cases in the survival data. And some will suggest that if the Psi hypothesis was not in any sense falsifiable, then so much the worse for the claim that it ever existed.

For all the above reasons, we need to have some independent empirical evidence (which is not to say, necessarily, laboratory evidence) for the existence of sneaky Psi in other contexts before we can appeal to it in order to explain those features of survival cases that do not fit into established (or confirmed) views about the limit of Psi. Until that occurs, it seems presumptuous and maximally implausible to assert that we might appeal successfully to Psi or

Super-Psi to explain, for example, the acquisition of unlearned skills (such as playing an instrument or speaking in an unlearned foreign language).

In the end, given Braude's (1989) admission that the existence of psi, or super-psi, is, as a cause at work in the survival cases, neither confirmable nor falsifiable by appeal to any factual evidence at all. It is difficult to see any explanation couched in terms of it as anything more than a merely logically possible explanation, no different in kind than offering explanations in terms of angels, godlings, and the gods of Homer, or Descartes' (1985) evil demon hypothesis, all of which are equally incapable of being empirically confirmed or falsified. Explanations in terms of such appeals are plausibly not explanations at all, because in not having any stateable test implications, they provide no predictions either.

Curiously enough, it is interesting that Braude (1992), more than anybody else, has argued (often convincingly, I believe), that in cases such as Joseph of Cupertino, D. D. Home, and Eusapia Palladino, we sample evidence for the existence of PK on a grand scale. It is difficult to see how we can accept as much and also argue that there is no way of confirming or falsifying that Psi exists. The natural inclination here is to grant that we do have strong evidence for the past existence of PK on a grand scale, but it is a long way from there to justifying the claim that it is Super-psi (or even dandy psi) at work in the survival cases when we want to explain behaviors that go beyond explanation in terms of ordinary Psi . . . especially, when we cannot, according to Braude (year), confirm or falsify such claims. Until we can do as much, appealing to Psi in order to explain the unusual data in these cases seems very much *ad hoc*, and unjustified, even if Super-Psi exists.

REPLY TO WHEATLEY

Wheatley's Rejection of Reincarnation

James M. O. Wheatley's (1995) review of my *Death and Personal Survival*, asserts that the book makes audacious claims, some of which he believes are extravagant. He thinks, for example, that my claim that it is irrational not to believe in some form of personal survival is "surely an overstatement." He also asserts that my proof that personal survival is neither logically impossible nor factually impossible is not altogether successful (294; Almeder 1992).

He also believes that it is incautious to claim that we can best explain the very rich reincarnation cases by "assuming that 'human personality' whatever it is, admits of reincarnation" (Wheatley 1995, 294). And finally, in commenting on the last chapter of the book which in part argues that personal survival is neither logically nor factually impossible, he says:

I do not find that anything in this book serves to counter Penelhum's argument that the idea that a bodiless person is logically incoherent (see Penelhum Especially 54–78), but Almeder does not insist that what survives is bodiless (though he seems to believe that personal survival without a body is a possibility). (Wheatley 1995, 294)

Let me respond to these criticisms.

To begin with, there is nothing at all "extravagant" about my claim that it is irrational not to believe in some form of post-mortem personal survival. Nor is it surely "an overstatement" to assert as much. But perhaps we have here a misunderstanding of what "irrational" means. When I say that Smith's belief is irrational, or that Smith is irrational for believing something or other, I need not mean that Smith is demonstrably insane in some clinical sense of the term, as if Smith were dysfunctional for being deluded in some belief and, for that reason, in need for psychiatric therapy of some sort. But not all forms of irrationality are forms of *insanity*. Even granting the difficulty of answering Bertrand Russell's (2009) famous question asking us to distinguish between a madman and an ardent supporter of an unpopular cause, insanity is a very special form of irrationality; but irrationality, understood in an *epistemic sense* means merely that someone's belief is demonstrably epistemically defective, and that one has no epistemic right to accept it. Similarly, when one says that it is irrational, after viewing all the arguments available, not to believe something or other, one can only mean that deliberate refusal to accept the belief in question is, given the force of the arguments involved, epistemically irresponsible in a very basic way.

Without caring to define here more fully the concept of rationality, nevertheless we can offer a preliminary criterion for determining whether one is acting irrationally in accepting or rejecting a belief of some sort:

> Minimally, one acts irrationally when one fails, after thoroughly viewing all the relevant evidence available, to accept a demonstrably sound argument (or proof) showing that something is so.

Admittedly, there is abundant research showing that people often cling to their beliefs even when the evidence for those beliefs is no longer available to them or is clearly refuted (13 Kahneman, etc.). In such cases we can, and do, say that their beliefs are irrational, and by this we merely mean to say that there is a serious epistemic defect running quite deeply in their thinking on the subject. Their beliefs are at variance with very strong evidence contrary to their beliefs. It does not mean that they are delusional rather than that they are strongly epistemically defective in believing what they do believe, given the evidence available against their beliefs. By implication, after closely examining all the evidence, it is, for example, irrational to believe that there never were any dinosaurs, or that people do not generally descend when they jump from tall buildings, or that the sun rotates around the earth, or that there are no muons.

Perhaps, I should not have used the word "irrational" when characterizing the beliefs of those who would not accept some form of *post-mortem* personal survival. Given the clinical sense of the term, I would certainly agree with Wheatley's (1995) view that the attribution of such irrationality to those who would not accept some form of personal *post-mortem* survival is extravagant and surely an overstatement. But given the *epistemic sense* of the word, that is, the sense that applies when people simply do not, or will not, accept a sound argument when it is presented to them, then the characterization is by no means extravagant or an overstatement. The only question is whether the argument for some form of personal *post-mortem* survival is so strong that rejecting it is a clear sign of epistemic irresponsibility unworthy of anyone seeking to satisfy minimally acceptable standards of rational belief. I argued at length that the answer to the question is "yes." Here again, not to accept the only plausible explanation available and fitting the best cases examined is irrational in the epistemic sense just characterized. Refuting such a claim depends on whether anybody has as plausible an explanation that does not require belief in some form of personal survival. If not, then it is not a matter of *assuming* that reincarnation is the best available explanation; it is a matter of having shown as much. So, there is nothing extravagant or incautious about the claim that it is irrational to disbelieve the evidence for *post-mortem* survival. That claim follows simply from the fact that, for the best cases examined, there is no available anti-survival explanation as plausible as the argument that explains the data in terms of some form of *post-mortem* personal survival.

But Wheatley (1995) also asserts that I failed to show altogether successfully that there is nothing logically impossible or factually impossible about post-mortem personal survival. In fact, he explains that there is nothing in the book to counter Terence Penelhum's (1974) "argument" that the idea of a bodiless person is logically incoherent (294).

In response, however, I examined closely and rejected Penelhum's argument in *Death and Personal Survival* (Almeder 1992, 83–85). There I urged, *inter alia*, that the concept of a bodiless person is logically incoherent *only if* one assumes or proves that it is a necessary truth that human personality is in some basic way identical with one's continued bodily existence, or that having a body is a necessary condition for being a person. Neither Penelhum, nor anybody else ever proved as much. So, Penelhum's (1974) position is a clear case of question-begging. The most people can say is that they cannot imagine what a bodiless person would, or could, be like; but that is not to prove, rather than to plead, what is at issue here.

There is certainly nothing logically impossible about human personality being in some important measure distinct from, and hence not completely reducible to, biochemical states of the body or brain, as we now know them.

It may be difficult to imagine what it would be like to be a bodiless person, but if we have learned anything at all from the followers of Socrates, Aristotle, Plato, Descartes, and many others believing in mind-body dualism (and minds as irreducible to properties of bodies) is by no means akin to believing in square circles. The idea of a square circle is incoherent (logically contradictory), but the idea of human personality, largely consisting in properties of a substance which while real (and probably sharing some properties in common with matter as we know it) is not identical with the physical body as we know it, and is not at all contradictory.

As I argued in the book, the explanation offered by C. D. Broad (1962) for what human personality must be like, and the nature of the mind and its interactions with the body, show very clearly that mind-body dualism is certainly not logically incoherent. The only way the idea of a bodiless person could be incoherent would be under the assumption that only physical objects (as we now understand them) exist and, as I have been urging, under that question-begging assumption we have no way to explain plausibly the data in the best cases for *post-mortem* survival (Almeder 1992, 262).

But perhaps, Penelhum and Wheatley, and others, believe that the incoherence here is not a matter of *logical incoherence*, that the idea of a bodiless person is *factually incoherent* rather than *logically incoherent*.

Well, if this sort of incoherence is what is meant, it can only amount to claiming that mind-body dualism, and what is required of it, must somehow deny what is factually necessary, and thus be logically inconsistent with well-established laws or theories, or basic principles of some sort. Along this line, some have suggested that if a bodiless personality could be an agent, causally interacting with the body (as we know it) and vice versa, then there would need to be a violation of the law of conservation of energy. In answering this objection, Broad (1962) was quick to note that the objection assumes that the only kind of causal interaction is that which involves a transfer of kinetic energy from one physical object to another. That in itself is what needs to be proven, namely that only physical objects, as we customarily understand them, exist.

Even so, it is to Broad's everlasting credit that he simply grants that a bodiless person would not be nothing; rather it would need to have, or in all likelihood would have, some properties that it shares in common with matter as we ordinarily understand it. In that way, causal interaction between bodies and the *bodiless person* can go forward without there needing to be a causal interaction between two bodies of the same type. In this way, no law of nature would be violated in defending the causalistic interaction of mind-body dualism.

Besides, Broad (1962) also claims that there is no logical nor factual incoherence with claiming that there is a basic kind of causality between two different kinds of items that cannot be totally understood by natural science alone, although one can verify that it exists simply by reflecting on one's own mental operations. So, it is difficult to see, for these reasons as well as the ones lay out in the book, how one could defend the view that the idea of a bodiless person is incoherent. It is certainly not logically impossible nor, for the reasons offered by Broad, is it factually impossible in any clear sense of what it would mean for a claim to be factually impossible. It may well be that a bodiless person is something whose causal activities, at least as a source of explaining human behavior, we would not understand in natural science; but that is no reason for thinking it factually impossible that such a causal interaction between bodies and bodiless persons cannot occur. However, appealing to that interaction to explain human behavior may well be unavailable to us. Whatever it is, a bodiless person is not nothing, and probably has some properties that we also find in physical bodies.

Wheatley (1995) also claims that it is incautious to believe that the best way to explain the very rich reincarnation cases is by "assuming" that "human personality (whatever it is) admits of reincarnation" (267). He defends this claim by observing a little later:

> As Almeder allows, we do not know what reincarnates, how it reincarnates, how long it reincarnates, whether it disappears after a series of reincarnations, or even why it reincarnates (p. 267). Do we nonetheless have a clear enough understanding of the concept of reincarnation to accord it the role of explaining cases of the sort Almeder discusses? I tend to doubt it. To say, with Almeder, that the survival hypothesis is now "strongly confirmed" (p. 269) or that not to believe in survival is "irrational" (p. xi) is at odds, it seems to me with the vagueness. Controversy, obscurity and confusion that marks the whole idea of 'life after death.' Such haziness, further, is one reason why I disagree with Almeder's claim that belief in reincarnation is at least as well-established as belief in the past existence of dinosaurs. Another reason is that dinosaur belief, at home as it is in the framework of paleontology, contrasts minimalist reincarnation tellingly in this respect with the belief in reincarnation, which is housed in no scientific theory at all. (Wheatley 1995, 296, quoting Almeder 1992)

In response, yes, I think we do know enough about personal minimalist reincarnation to allow the belief to explain the richer cases discussed above. We may not know how such reincarnation occurs, or why, or for how long, but, again, that is perfectly consistent with knowing that it occurs. We only need to know that a sufficient criterion for personal identity is continuity of memory, or that what we should and would accept as sufficient evidence for somebody being the reincarnation of Julius Caesar, for example, is that apart from claiming that he remembers having lived as Julius Caesar, he would have had most of the memories that we would expect Julius Caesar to have, and confirmed personal memories that only Caesar could have had. My argument was, in part, that if somebody did show up with all those memories and claimed to be Julius Caesar reincarnated, there is available to us no plausible way to explain his having those memories if we do not explain it by appealing to personal reincarnation.

And to say that some people have reincarnated from time to time is not to appeal to a vague, obscure, or confused concept. It is to say, rather simply that human personality is not totally identifiable with properties of the human body as we know it, and that it survives biological death as the repository of certain mental states and dispositions having to do with memory, intelligence, sense of humor, and acquired cognitive skills; and that it enters another bodily form some time later in order to continue its existence as a human being. There is nothing vague, obscure or confused about the claim that *whatever I am, I am not completely identifiable with my body; I may therefore survive my biological death with more or less the memories I now have and with the mental dispositions I now have, and continue my existence after a while in another body, in which I will acquire additional beliefs and dispositions.*

What makes such a claim controversial is that it is difficult to imagine surviving as a causal agent in this world without having a physical body. Bear in mind also that in the history of natural science we often get solid evidence for a fact but do not know how or even why it occurs. It is fair to say, for example, that a certain number of cases of primary schizophrenia were known to be purely genetic or metabolic, as a result of identical twin studies, long before we could identify the gene causing the disease and the mechanism by which the gene produced the disease. In those days, it was not uncommon to hear geneticists say: "We do not know what gene or complex of genes causes it, how such genes work, or why such genes are there at all. But we do know that it is sometimes a purely genetic disease because there is no other equally plausible way to explain the results of the identical twin studies."

As it happens, for the above reasons, we knew long before the discovery of the gene(s) causing primary schizophrenia, and long before we knew how the gene works in producing the disease that a certain percentage of the cases of primary schizophrenia were in fact of a purely genetic origin. So, I am arguing here for much the same considerations or reasons that we know that some persons have reincarnated. There is no more plausible explanation for the data in the richest cases.

Wheatley (1995) claims in the section quoted above, moreover, "that it is because of the haziness surrounding the whole idea of '*life after death*'" (296; emphasis mine), that he doubts that reincarnation is at least as well established as belief in past existence of dinosaurs. Another reason that he offers is that the dinosaur belief, at home as it is in paleontology, contrasts tellingly with the belief in reincarnation which is housed in no scientific theory at all.

As I understand it, Stevenson (1978), for example, is simply trying to explain the ostensibly unusual behavior of the people in the richer cases, in much the same way Freud was trying to explain certain forms of hysterical behavior by appealing to the hypothesis of the subconscious. For Stevenson, the behaviors in question have no better or plausible explanation as the belief in reincarnation.

As long as the hypothesis is empirically confirmable and falsifiable, in the way indicated in the book, it makes little difference where we end up placing it in natural science.

Finally, Wheatley (1995) says that I oversimplify Ayer's views on Reincarnation. He cites the following from Ayer's (1963) *The Concept of a Person and Other Essays*, which appeared in the same year the hardback volume of Ayer's (1956) *The Problem of Knowledge* appeared:

> even if someone could convince us that he ostensibly remembered the experiences of a person long since dead, and . . . this was backed by an apparent continuity of character, I think that we should prefer to say that he had somehow picked up the dead man's memories and dispositions rather than that he was the same person in another body; the idea of a person's leading a discontinuous existence in time as well as in space is just that much more fantastic. (Ayer 1963, 127)

In retrospect, Ayer (1956) was tempted to argue in *The Problem of Knowledge*; that the reincarnation of Julius Caesar would be that the person in question has all the personal memories we would expect of Caesar, and memories that only Caesar could have had. The person must also *claim* to be the reincarnation of Julius Caesar; he utters such sentences as "I remember being Julius Caesar in my last life." But it is also fair to say that Ayer does not non-equivocally endorse the view that if someone were to present such evidence, then we would have clear and noncontroversial evidence for reincarnation. He says that it would call for a decision on our part. But he does make it clear that personal identity would be a matter of having certain personal memories rather than bodily traits or bodily continuity. It may be fair to say that Ayer waffled on what should count as evidence for reincarnation, but he allows that there would be nothing unjustified in believing in reincarnation if somebody with many of Julius Caesar's personal memories (and a few other mental traits) showed up on the scene (529–33). Like Parfit (1984), Ayer thought it is not much of an issue because he thought that nobody in fact has ever turned up with such memories. But they both seem to agree that if somebody were to show up with such traits, then belief in reincarnation would not be inappropriate.

Even so, there seems to be a contradiction in the passage just quoted from Ayer (1956), simply because one cannot conceivably *pick up* a dead man's memories and dispositions without thereby becoming that person if the criterion of personal identity, which Ayer (1995) defends in the *Problem of Knowledge*, is to be accepted; and I have argued that that criterion should be accepted. "*The same person in another body*" just means having all the memories we would expect of that person (and some memories that only that person could have had) and mental dispositions of the dead man (Ayer 1963, 127; emphasis mine). The point here is that if I had most of the personal memories of Julius Caesar, and some personal memories that only Julius Caesar could have had, and if I claim to remember, in virtue of these memories, having lived as Julius Caesar, then I am Julius Caesar reincarnated, although to be sure, I may be more than that also. If I had all those properties that would be sufficient for saying that I am, in part, Julius Caesar reincarnated. It cannot be correct to describe me as somehow picking-up the dead man's memories and dispositions, but not being the person in which Julius Caesar has reincarnated. Otherwise, nothing would count for anybody ever being reincarnated, and that, by implication, is to declare *a-priori, that belief in personal reincarnation is false.*

So, it will not do, by way of offering an alternative explanation for some of the richer reincarnation cases discussed and described in earlier pages, to simply say "He somehow picked up the memories and mental dispositions of Julius Caesar (as well as a few other traits that only Caesar could have had). But Julius Caesar is not really reincarnated in this man." That alternative interpretation of that data (whoever offers it) is consistent with adopting a criterion of personal identity only in terms of bodily continuity; and while Ayer (1956; 1963) has argued against the latter, it is not at all clear that the position he finally adopts is as squarely consistent with the criterion for personal identity he in fact adopts. Presumably, at any rate, the historical point is not as crucial as the logical point that personal identity cannot be explicated in terms of bodily continuity.

A METHODOLOGICAL OBJECTION

It may be helpful to repeat, and to elaborate more briefly upon a fairly pervasive methodological objection. Perhaps the most popular or pervasive criticism of the case studies offered and discussed in *Death and Personal Survival*, is that there is altogether too much inductive evidence of fraud, delusion, hoax, or simple deception in the history of the paranormal to justify generalizing from what seems to be persuasive cases studies to conclusions supportive of some form of personal survival. In *Death and Personal Survival* this objection emerged when examining Susan Blackmore's (1982) analysis of the Out-of-Body Experience (OBE) material, and also in the last chapter under the heading of "The Long Shadow of Hoax and Fraud" (see Almeder 1992). The short answer to the objection is that the richer cases are different in that they deny an analysis in terms of fraud, hoax, delusion, or simple deception; and hence are, as a class, logically distinct from those that would be unacceptable as evidence.

And it is not simply that in these richer cases we have not yet found the fraud, deceit, or delusion that must be there. The analysis of the cases offered as evidence (especially in the areas of reincarnation and OBE) shows that the richer cases are not at all like those cases that have in the past turned out to be fraudulent or defective. Let the richer cases carry the burden of evidence, speak for themselves, and let those who think that they fall inductively into the class of fraudulent cases show that these cases warrant being placed into that category. Failure to do as much amounts to nothing more than an *a-priori* claim that nothing can count as empirical evidence for some form of personal *post-mortem* survival, when in fact what is being argued is that these cases should count.

Even if we admit that historically most claims about the paranormal, when examined closely, have been shown to be unworthy of rational acceptance, it by no means follows that we have examined the large number of distinctive ones that do not fall into that class. If most people die who jump off the Brooklyn Bridge, it by no means follows that everybody will die who jumps off the Brooklyn Bridge; and if some people survive the jump, we need to find an explanation of that unusual fact, rather than deny it as if most reported cases of the paranormal have turned out to be unacceptable as evidence for reasons of fraud, delusion, deception, and sloppy methodology, it has not been shown in all cases (or even the majority of cases) are unacceptable for those reasons.

By analogy, some of us have been trying to show that the richer cases are more numerous than generally supposed or reported, and in fact, like those people who jump off the Brooklyn Bridge and survive, it would be appropriate to put these cases beyond the pale of an inductive generalization from defective cases. These cases need to be explained, rather than summarily dismissed because they bear superficial similarities to those past cases that have been instances of fraud, deceit, deception, hoax, or sloppy methodology. And as we contend, the only plausible explanation that fits with the facts is some form of *post-mortem personal survival*. Before we reject these richer cases as solid evidence for some form of *post-mortem* survival, surely somebody needs to show that they are defective in the way that others have been shown to be defective in the past.

Finally, by way of a footnote on the above, and offered by Braude (1992a), who claims that his position is often not properly understood by those who take issue with it. Sometimes he urges that he is not trying to offer a competing explanation for the data in strong reincarnation cases, or other survival cases. Rather he is only arguing that "the plausibility of the super-psi-hypothesis is such that there are fewer reasons to reject it in these cases than commentators usually suppose" and that his point is basically to show that "super-psi" explanations have been underrated and misunderstood, not that they are either clearly or even marginally preferable (127–44; see also Braude 1992b, 151). This seems to suggest that under the best of circumstances the *Super-Psi hypothesis* must be at least as plausible an explanation of the data in the best cases as is the hypothesis of survival. Any weaker claim about the value of *Super-Psi* as an alternative plausible explanation for such data would not seem to warrant serious consideration.

Chapter 4

Where Are We Now?

BRIEF REVIEW OF EARLIER PARTS

We saw in chapter 1 that *Physicalism* asserts that the *only* objects in this majestic and mysterious universe are *physical objects* or *material substances*, governed by the laws of physics and natural selection. Interestingly however, nobody has yet shown, proved, or justifiably accepted the existence of immaterial substances because physicalists say that there are demonstrably no *immaterial substances*.

So, physicalists (also known as reductive materialists) typically *assume* that immaterial substances do not exist. And they offer the five core objections we examined *against* belief in the existence of immaterial substances.

We also saw in chapter 1 that physicalists (or reductive materialists) propose the five different arguments *against* believing in, and showing that there are no Cartesian Immaterial Substances. Those core arguments we examined carefully and rejected them.

Those core objections or arguments *against* believing in Cartesian Mind-Body Dualism are fundamental. The *belief* in the existence of immaterial substances is indefensible because:

1. It is not empirically testable or confirmable;
2. It is in principle testable and confirmable but unconfirmed; (Parfit)
3. It is testable and confirmable, but shown to be false; (Searle)
4. It is unnecessary to explain anything;
5. It cannot serve to explain anything; (Levine)

After examining these five core objections, we concluded that each of the five failed remarkably as objections for the various reasons indicated in this book, and so the natural sciences have not refuted Cartesian Mind-Body

Dualism because *mental events are not physical objects*. So, presumably, these are currently the best available objections our materialists and physicalists can offer. Furthermore, the promise of reductive materialism to explain human personality, mental events, consciousness, desires, feeling pain, feeling love, feeling happiness or sadness, and behavior is unlikely ever to be fulfilled. These mental events can *cause* physical overt behaviors, even though these mental events are not physical objects capable of transferring kinetic energy to physical objects. They are *immaterial substances* that somehow transfer kinetic energy to other physical objects without being physical objects themselves. How can this happen? More on this later.

MENTAL CAUSATION AND CONSCIOUSNESS

In chapter 2, we also focused on a concerted effort during the last fifty years to provide the increasingly relevant data emerging from carefully examined personal reincarnation case studies and published for reasons of justifying Cartesian Mind-Body Dualism. If those reasons are clearly convincing, the compelling data derives from robust empirical evidence or studies available that some persons have indeed reincarnated, as we noted, for example, in "The Case of the Third James" and in "The Case for Personal Reincarnation," and among other cases discussed.

We called it "A Minimalist Reincarnation Theory." We also call it a "minimalist hypothesis" because it tells us so little about the nature of this strange, mysterious non-physical property or "stuff" essential to some persons after biological death.

Also we suggested above that this *stuff* is the equivalence of Cartesian "Immaterial Substances" having certain cognitive, volitional, and emotive characteristics. Some of the most important case studies described in chapter 2 are crucial over the years in providing many published case studies for research scientists and distinguished scholars, in related labs at respected universities, such as the University of Virginia, in medical schools focusing on medical studies, and for other scholars advancing and publishing in those related natural sciences, including psychiatry.

Again, this minimalist hypothesis does not assert that *ALL* human beings reincarnate at some time or other. We have no empirical evidence for that claim. Also this hypothesis does not profess to inform us *why* or *how* this process occurs, where these immaterial substances live after death, and what they do before reincarnating into another body with a sound memory of some things that he buried but that nobody else knows where he alone clearly buried some physical items that only he can now verify and which only he knows something that he remembers something now and nobody else knew or knows.

Nor, as also described, does it show how often this process of reincarnation occurs, where it occurs, when and whether there is some definite end or point to the process, and why exactly does it occur at all? Why do some persons reincarnate and others not? What do they? What is the point of it all? The above process does not imply that every aspect of each human that reincarnates whenever that person reincarnates, but only what is essential to the personality in question, namely only that which would be empirically sufficient to identify the person as distinct from any other person.

As we also discerned, when some humans survive biological death, what survives is a *person* without a body and ostensibly not a physical object able to convey kinetic energy to another physical object.

This leaves us with *reductive materialism* or physicalism and "immaterial substances" incapable of transferring kinetic energy to any physical objects. More on this anon.

JAEGWON KIM

In the opening page of his excellent book *Physicalism, or Something Near Enough*, Jaegwon Kim (2005) introduced the two principal challenges confronting contemporary physicalism. He said the following:

> The problem of mental causation is to explain how mentality can have a causal role in a world that is fundamentally physical. The supervenience/exclusion argument shows that within a physicalist scheme, mental causation is possible only if mental phenomena are physically reducible. But is the mental reducible to the physical? In particular, can we give a reductive physicalist account of consciousness? This is the problem of consciousness. There are well-known, though by no means uncontested, reasons for thinking that phenomenal, or qualitative, consciousness cannot be physically reduced. In this way the two issues, mental causation and consciousness, become interlocked: The problem of mental causation is solvable only if mentality is physically reducible. However, phenomenal consciousness resists physical reduction, putting its causal efficacy in peril. (Kim 2005, 7–18)

...

> It is difficult to imagine how "immaterial minds" or material things could causally affect each other. By eliminating immaterial substances we establish ontological physicalism-the thesis that bits of matter and their aggregates exhaust the contents of the world. . . . If mental properties are to retain their causal efficacy they must be reducible to physical properties. Reductive explanation of

mentality apparently requires the derivation of psychological statements from statements about neural/physical states and processes. How can this be accomplished? (Kim 2005, 30–31)

In any event, the important feature of this personal minimalist reincarnation theory, or hypothesis, is that it shows empirically testable, falsifiable, and confirmed as the best available empirical explanation of the data, and who claims to be reincarnated in a large number of the best case studies of people who sincerely believe that they are indeed reincarnated.

There are similar cases where we find that the evidence in these reincarnation case studies support belief in material substances. But to be sure, they also support belief in "immaterial substances" providing causal effects for transferring kinetic energy from one physical object to another. A good example is "The Case of the Third James." This is what Jaegwon Kim affirmed above when he said:

> There are well-known, though by no means uncontested, reasons for thinking that phenomenal, or qualitative, consciousness cannot be physically reduced. In this way the two issues, mental causation and consciousness, become interlocked: the problem of mental causation is solvable only if mentality is physically reducible; however, phenomenal consciousness resists physical reduction, putting its causal efficacy in peril. (Kim 2005, 7–18)

More on this later.

Incidentally, back in 1990, Dr. Ian Stevenson informed me, in writing, that there were important files on reincarnation studies for research with about 2,400 case studies housed from 1974 in the Division of Parapsychology at the Medical School Library in the University of Virginia; and today there are as many as 3,000 case studies available for psychiatrists and other scientists—most of them are from the United States, Australia, England, Western Europe, Israel, France, Lebanon, India, and Africa.

Doubtless, some scientists will simply reject the belief in personal reincarnation even as an empirically verifiable hypothesis. They believe rather that belief in personal reincarnation is basically a religious belief of some sort, or philosophical gibberish, or superstitious hocus-pocus. Some even believe that the hypothesis is absurd, worthy of ridicule, and incoherent to the core. Very few will probably believe that it might be empirically verifiable under the methods of testing and confirmation in the natural sciences, much less *de facto* confirmed empirically.

In chapter 2, we also updated and polished thought experiments and six case studies, both of which are important to show the empirical conditions necessary and sufficient for showing, successfully, that personal reincarnation does exist and that suitable evidence is available documenting that some people can, and have, personally reincarnated. If these selectively empirical case studies are persuasive, they will provide clear evidence that Immaterial Substances must exist and have existed, thereby to provide a strong scientifically empirical case for rejecting Physicalism or Reductive Materialism based on the compelling evidence.

Chapter 2 also examines and rejects, several critics and possible consequences with a little help from the works of C. D. Broad, Joseph Levine, Richard Swinburne, Jaegwon Kim, Sidney Shoemaker, Bernard Williams, A. J. Ayer, Derek Parfit, Christine Ladd Franklin, Bertrand Russell, Dr. James Tucker, Sarah Thomason, Terrence Penelhum, Terry Horgan, Ian Stevenson, Steve Braude, and David Chalmers.

DANIEL DENNETT

Many philosophers, scientists, physicists, theologians, and distinguished scholars have worked valiantly indeed to find sufficient empirical evidence to rest comfortably in the various arguments for accepting the theory of Reductive Materialism. So, as we will see below, Dennett's (1982; 1991/2000; 2005) arguments led him to the view that there are no Cartesian "immaterial substances" and no human consciousness, at least as many will think about it. He endorses the view that human consciousness is *simply a false by-product of the workings of the brain and produces neurologically and biologically all other mental states that flow from, and cause, various neural effects allowing human behaviors that would not otherwise appear.* The important point is that the brain produces from its own mysterious resources the wherewithal to produce biological and neurological effects necessary to flourish under natural selection. See now how Dennett (2005) elaborates in his delightful book, *Sweet Dreams: Philosophical Obstacles to a Science of Consciousness* (see 71–79).

In *Sweet Dreams*, Dennett (2005) notes convincingly that Robert Wright worries about Dennett's story on consciousness, and he is not alone. Dennett quotes Wright's (2000) view clearly, when Wright said:

> Of course, the Problem here is with the claim that consciousness is "identical" to physical brain states. The more Dennett and others try to explain to me what they mean by this, the more convinced I became is that what they really mean is that consciousness does not exist. (Wright 2000, quoted in Dennett 2005, chap. 21, n14)

This coincides with what Dennett (1991/2000) said earlier:

as I have argued at length (1991, and in many subsequent papers), this imagined showcase, the Cartesian Theater, where everything comes together for consciousness, must be dismantled. All the work done by the imagined homunculus in the Cartesian Theater must be distributed among various lesser agencies in the brain, none of which is conscious. Whenever that step is taken, however, the Subject vanishes, replaced by mindless bits of machinery executing their task. Can this be the right direction for the theory of consciousness to take? (Dennett 2005, 69)

Here opinion is strikingly divided. On the one hand, there are those who join me in recognizing that if you leave the subject in your theory, you have not yet begun! A good theory of consciousness should make a conscious mind look like an abandoned factory (recall Leibniz's mill) full of humming machinery and nobody home to supervise it, or to enjoy it, or to witness it.

On the other hand, some people hate this idea. Jerry Fodor (1998) writes in his *In Critical Condition: Polemical Essays on Cognitive Science and the Philosophy of Mind*, for instance: "If, in short, there is a community of computers living in my head, there had also better be somebody who is in charge; and by God, it had better be me" (207).

THE LAST STORY ON "QUALIA"

We can remember that many philosophers noted that Jaegwon Kim, for example, like many others, struggled with the concept of "qualia"; and that he came to believe that "qualia" are simply "the qualitative aspects of mental states" but are clearly caused by physical states and to physical properties that could not easily reduce to physical properties of brain states. This issue led Kim (2005) to examine the concept of "Supervenience." His work took him to a detailed study of the concept of causation, a central concept of metaphysics (see also Kim and Sosa 1999). After this, his pressing question was, how can we support a commitment to the causal closure of physics, that is, our assumption that there is in principal an adequate physical explanation of any event in the physical world and still maintain the causal significance of mental events, that is, that they are not just epiphenomenal consciousness of physical events, but play a genuine role in determining subsequent events in the theory of knowledge? Kim criticized "naturalized epistemology" a la Quine, insisting that on purely descriptive belief-forming practices that have traditionally been taken cannot account for the justification of knowledge claims, although constructing a theory of such justification (see Kim 2005, 198).

THE LAST WORD—POSSIBLY

Let me say briefly that chapter 2 shows that some people have reincarnated. We find the best minimalist reincarnation cases, when studied seriously, are compelling especially in cases such as "The Case of the Third James," or even the thought experiments including the essay "Julius Caesar on a Park Bench," along with several similar cases.

Seemingly crucial in such cases is that the subject is usually a young person claiming to have lived in a past life many years earlier in another place, in this case ones that she remembers and describes in many details. Moreover, these subjects provide detailed information about that past life, their name, and memories about different persons and events that the subject clearly remembers. Among such memories, this subject in particular claims to remember where she hid money and shoes, and twenty gifts from her mother, and other things she buried secretly during the night and that she could now tell them where the buried treasure was hidden, say a hundred years ago. And where the subject was hanged for killing his brother. The brother was buried with some gold in a hidden graveyard one hundred miles away in a small village where the subject exhumed the body buried with his treasures.

So we can confirm empirically the subject's memory claims of a remote and past life if what she claims to remember we can find something today buried in the ground, for example, that we would have expected to find if her memory claims were demonstrably true.

How does the subject remember today demonstrably certain events or people that occurred from the time she died so long ago? The cause of her current reliable memories of things confirmed that happened so long ago may well be an immaterial substance event, such as a mental substance causing a material substance or a physical object.

In the end, consciousness seems to be an Immaterial Substance of some sort, if it exists at all, and not a physical object. Legions of philosophers and natural scientists have spent, and continue to spend, much time examining and writing about the nature and effects of consciousness, and about the meaning of "qualia." But we can do our best to wait for more written on these ultimately difficult topics to comprehend for philosophers and scientists.

As indicated back in the Foreword, the mind-body problem, as it currently exists, is simply a matter of successfully determining who has the right answer on whether materialism is correct, or whether non-materialist is correct.

As I argued that materialism, or physicalism, was and is committed to the view that *the only objects in this world are physical objects and that there are no "immaterial substances."*

But nobody has yet shown, or proven, that there are not any "immaterial substances." It is an assumption on the part of physicalists. *But there are mental events* such as being conscious, feeling pain, joy, happiness, sadness, desiring, thinking, wondering, feeling dreadful, loving, loosing something or someone cherished, feeling the taste of a wonderful meal, or viewing a sunset, or feeling depressed, and so on. *All of these are cognitive mental events.* They are not physical objects but they can and do have causal effects on other physical objects. *Such mental events can convey kinetic energy without there being physical objects themselves.*

After the crucial examination of the empirical evidence offered in this book to the effect that some people have demonstrably reincarnated, over a long period of time without a body, and thereby have existed with memories and without the brain for quite some time before they reincarnated. *This brings us back to immaterial substances as cognitive and mental events retained after bodily death without being a physical object conveying kinetic energy to another physical object.*

This seems to be a good finish here for a good story. I am also sure that I must have made serious errors along the way and hope they will not be judged too egregious. I will be grateful for any kindly criticisms where necessary.

Appendix

A. J. Ayer on Personal Reincarnation

The British philosopher A. J. Ayer confronted the possibility of personal reincarnation after he raised the question of whether human consciousness can survive biological death (Ayer 1956, chap. 5; see also Ayer 1963). Toward the end of his interesting essay "The Concept of a Person" (Ayer 1963, 127), and after he had argued that bodily continuity was certainly necessary and sufficient for determining personal identity, he said:

> even if someone could convince us that he ostensibly remembered the experiences of a person who is long since dead, and even if this were backed by an apparent continuity of character, I think that we should prefer to say that he had picked up the dead man's memories and dispositions rather than that he was the same person in another body; the idea of a person's leading a discontinuous existence in time as well as in space is just that much more fantastic! Nevertheless, I think that it would be open to us to admit the logical possibility of reincarnation merely by laying down the rule that if a person who is physically identified as living at a later time does have the ostensible memories and character of a person who is physically identified as living at an earlier time, they are to be counted as one person and not two. For given that this condition is satisfied, the question of their numerical identity is a matter for decision and not a question of fact. (Ayer 1963, 127–28)

Here Ayer (1963) asserts that the criterion for personal identity is simply a matter of physical continuity. For various reasons he has argued in different places that one's identity as a person is tied to having the same body that continues to exist throughout a life of physical changes. So, physical continuity is at least a necessary condition, or a major criterion, for being the unique person each of us is. Our experiences are thus parasitic on our continuing and biological bodies.

However, in the above highlighted text Ayer also grants that there are subsidiary criteria of personal identity, and these are criteria of memory and of continuity of character. Ayer then moves to the question of reincarnation, noting that if anybody could convince him that somebody ostensibly remembers the personal experiences of a person long since dead, and if this was backed by continuity of character, Ayer would allow us to accept the belief in personal reincarnation.

But even so, Ayer (1963) would still prefer rather to say that he (the allegedly reincarnated subject) had somehow mysteriously picked-up the dead man's memories and dispositions rather than that he was the same person in another body; the idea of a person's leading a discontinuous existence in time as well as in space is just that much more fantastic (127).

So, by way of a brief assessment of Ayer's (1963) position in the above cited text, Ayer is willing to grant that reincarnation is logically possible just in case somebody could convince him (Ayer) that somebody verifiably remembers the personal experiences of a person long since dead, and if this were backed by continuity of character (127).

Ayer repeats saying that he has no problem with accepting the logical possibility of reincarnation simply if we lay down a rule that if a person who is identified as living at a later time does have the ostensible memories and character of a person who is physically living at an earlier time, they are to be counted as one person and not two.

In summary, Ayer (1963) in this essay does not give us leave to believe in reincarnation, but only in the logical possibility of reincarnation, and then if only we lay down a rule to the effect that if a person living at a later time has the ostensible memories and character of the person who physically lived at an earlier time, they are to be counted as one person and not two. Not only does Ayer not give us clear permission to believe in personal reincarnation, he would much rather prefer to say that the person having the personal memories of another person long since dead somehow miraculously picked up the dead man's memories and dispositions rather than that he was the same person in another body.

Ayer, incidentally, gave us no reason to suppose that some humans might be able to mysteriously pick-up a dead man's personal memories and dispositions without being that person. He provides no empirical evidence for justifying that preferred supposition. And why lay down a rule, rather than provide a sound argument for the claim that if we suddenly came across somebody who demonstrably has some of the personal memories of George Washington, verified memories that only Washington could have had, we should prefer to think instead that he mysteriously picked up those memories rather than that he was George Washington reincarnated?[1]

NOTES

1. Elsewhere, in Ayer's (1956) *The Problem of Knowledge* (193–96ff), he sees nothing contradictory about the possibility of personal reincarnation. Here he says that if Julius Caesar's personal memories about personal events known only to Julius Cesar are revealed by a living human in great detail and are subsequently shown to be true, then Ayer professes that he would not know what to say. He grants that the living person claiming to be Julius Caesar might *really* be Julius Caesar. He thinks that is a rational decision, but he prefers to think that the fellow claiming to be Caesar also might have had some mysterious powers of being able to access Caesar's memories without being Caesar. In the end, Ayer affirms that the question of reincarnation calls for a decision that might be most useful and not a matter of fact. He waffled. In any event he was steadfastly committed to bodily continuity as the primary criterion for personal identity and that therefore it seems impossible that we should end up with the concept of a "person" extending to some non-physical substance not unlike a Cartesian immaterial substance.

Ayer seemingly admits here that the criterion for personal identity is simply a matter of physical continuity. For various reasons he has argued in different places that one's identity as a person is tied to having the same body that continues to exist throughout a life of physical changes. So, physical continuity is at least a necessary condition, or a major criterion, for being the unique person each of us is. Our experiences are thus parasitic on our continuing and biological bodies. However, in the above highlighted text Ayer also grants that there are subsidiary criteria of personal identity, and these are criteria of memory and continuity of character.

Ayer repeats saying that he has no problem with accepting the logical possibility of reincarnation simply if we lay down a rule that if a person who is identified as living at a later time does have the ostensible memories and character of a person who is physically living at an earlier time, they are to be counted as one person and not two.

Accordingly, Ayer, in this essay, does not give us permission to believe in reincarnation, but only belief in the *logical possibility of reincarnation*, and even then *if only we lay down a rule* to the effect that if a person living at a later time has the personal memories and character of the person who physically lived at an earlier time, they are to be counted as one person and not two. In any event, Ayer gives us no reason to suppose that some humans might be able to mysteriously pick up a dead man's personal memories and dispositions without being that person. He gives us no empirical evidence for that supposition.

References

Almeder, Robert. 1988. "Response to 'Past Tongues Remembered?'" *Skeptical Inquirer* 12, no. 3 (Spring): 321–23, https://skepticalinquirer.org/1988/04/response-to-past-tongues-remembered/.

Almeder, Robert. 1992. *Death and Personal Survival: The Evidence for Life After Death.* Lanham, MD: Littlefield Adams.

Almeder, Robert. 1994. Review of *The Rediscovery of the Mind*, by John Searle. *Journal of Scientific Exploration*, 420–24.

Almeder, Robert. 1996a. "Recent Responses to Survival Research." *Journal of Scientific Exploration* 10, no. 4 (December): 495–517.

Almeder, Robert. 1996b. "Almeder's Reply to Wheatley & Braude." *Journal of Scientific Exploration* 10, no. 4 (December): 529–33.

Almeder, Robert. 1998. *Harmless Naturalism: The Limits of Science and the Nature of Philosophy.* Chicago: Open Court.

Almeder, Robert. 2001. "On Reincarnation: A Reply to Hales." *Philosophia* 28, nos. 1–4 (June): 347–58. https://doi.org/10.1007/BF02379785.

Ayer, A. J. [Alfred Jules]. 1956. *The Problem of Knowledge.* London: Penguin Books.

Ayer, A. J. 1963. *The Concept of a Person and Other Essays.* New York: St. Martin's Press.

Ayer, A. J. 1994. "On Making Philosophy Intelligible." In *Metaphysics and Common Sense*, by A. J. Ayer, 1–17. Sudbury, MA: Jones and Bartlett.

Blackmore, Susan J. 1982. *Beyond the Body: An Investigation of Out-of-Body Experiences.* London: Heinemann.

Braude, Stephen E. 1986. *The Limits of Influence: Psychokinesis and the Philosophy of Science.* Abingdon-on-Thames, UK: Routledge & Kegan Paul.

Braude, Stephen E. 1989. "Evaluating the Super-Psi Hypothesis." In *Exploring the Paranormal: Perspectives on Belief and Experience*, edited by George K. Zollschan, John F. Shoemaker, and G. F. Jerry Walsh, 25–38. Dorset, UK: Prism Press.

Braude, Stephen E. 1992a. "Survival or Super-Psi?" *Journal of Scientific Exploration* 6, no. 2 (June): 127–44.

Braude, Stephen E. 1992b. "Reply to Stevenson." *Journal of Scientific Exploration* 6, no. 2 (June): 127–44.

References

Broad, C. D. [Charles Dunbar]. 1925. *Mind and Its Place in Nature*. London: Routledge and Kegan Paul.

Broad, C. D. 1962. *Lectures on Psychical Research*. New York: Humanities Press.

Chalmers, David J. 1996. *The Conscious Mind*. Oxford: Oxford University Press.

Davis, Dorothy. 1970. *History of Harrison County, West Virginia*. Edited by Elizabeth Sloan. Clarksburg, WV: American Association of University Women.

Dennett, Daniel C. 1982. "How to Study Consciousness Empirically; or Nothing Comes to Mind." *Syntheses* 53, no. 2 (November): 159–80. http://hdl.handle.net/10427/56702.

Dennett, Daniel C. 1991/2000. *Consciousness Explained*. Cambridge, MA: MIT Press.

Dennett, Daniel C. 2005. *Sweet Dreams: Philosophical Obstacles to a Science of Consciousness*. Cambridge, MA: MIT Press.

Descartes, René. 1985. *The Philosophical Writings Of Descartes*. 2 vols. Translated by John Cottingham, Roberts Stoothoth, and Dugald Murdoch. Cambridge: Cambridge University Press.

Edwards, Paul. 2011. *Reincarnation: A Critical Examination*. Buffalo, NY: Prometheus Books.

Flew, A. G. N. [Antony Garrard Newton]. 1956. "Can a Man Witness His Own Funeral?" *Hibbert Journal* 54 (January): 242–50.

Fodor, Jerry A. 1998. *In Critical Condition: Polemical Essays on Cognitive Science and the Philosophy of Mind*. Cambridge, MA: MIT Press.

Guirdham, Arthur. 1970. *The Cathars and Reincarnation*. London, UK: Neville Spearman.

Hales, Steven D. 2001a. "Evidence and the Afterlife." *Philosophia* 28, nos. 1-4 (June): 335–46. https://doi.org/10.1007/BF02379784.

Hales, Steven D. 2001b. "Reincarnation Redux." *Philosophia* 28, nos. 1-4 (June): 359–67. https://doi.org/10.1007/BF02379786.

Harris, Melvin. 1986. "Are 'Past-Life' Regressions Evidence of Reincarnation?" *Free Inquiry* 6 (Fall): 18–23. https://cdn.centerforinquiry.org/wp-content/uploads/sites/26/1986/10/22161022/p18.pdf.

Hempel, Carl G. 1966. *Philosophy of Natural Science*. Englewood Cliffs, NJ: Prentice Hall.

Horgan, Terry. 2006. Review of *Purple Haze: The Puzzle of Consciousness*, by Joseph Levine, *NoÛs* 40, no. 3: 579–88.

Kim, Jaegwon. 2005. *Physicalism, or Something Near Enough*. Princeton Monographs in Philosophy. Princeton, NJ: Princeton University Press.

Kim, Jaegwon, and Ernest Sosa, eds. 1999. *Metaphysics: An Anthology*. Oxford: Blackwell.

Levine, Joseph. 2001. Purple Haze: The Problem of Consciousness. Oxford: Oxford University Press.

Parfit, Derek. 1971a. "Personal Identity." Philosophical Review 80, no. 1 (January): 3–27. http://www.jstor.org/stable/2184309.

Parfit, Derek. 1971b. On "The Importance of Self-Identity." Journal of Philosophy 68, no. 20 (October): 683–90. https://doi.org/10.2307/2024939.

Parfit, Derek. 1984. Reasons and Persons. Oxford: Oxford University Press.
Parfit, Derek. 2001. "Personal Identity." In Metaphysics: Contemporary Readings, edited by Michael J. Loux, 374–95. London: Routledge.
Penelhum, Terence. 1970. Survival and Disembodied Existence. New York: Humanities Press.
Reid, Thomas. 1785/1969 *Essays on the Intellectual Powers of Man*. Reprint. Cambridge, MA: MIT Press.
Rorty, Richard. 1965. "Mind-Body Identity, Privacy, and Categories." *Review of Metaphysics* 19, no. 1 (September): 24–54. http://www.jstor.org/stable/20124096.
Russell, Bertrand. 2009. *Human Knowledge: Its Scope and Limits*. Oxfordshire, UK: Taylor & Francis.
Searle, John R. 1992. The Rediscovery of the Mind. Cambridge, MA: MIT Press.
Searle, John R. 2004. Interview "Toward a Unified Theory of Reality." Harvard Review of Philosophy 12 (Spring): 93–113. https://philarchive.org/archive/GANAIT-2v1.
Shoemaker, Sydney. 1970. "Persons and Their Pasts." American Philosophical Quarterly 7, no. 4 (October): 269–85. https://www.jstor.org/stable/20009360.
Stevenson, Ian. 1974. Xenoglossy: A Review and Report of a Case. Charlottesville: University Press of Virginia.
Stevenson, Ian. 1975. Cases of the Reincarnation Type. Volume 1: Ten Cases in India. Charlottesville: University Press of Virginia.
Stevenson, Ian. 1978. *Twenty Cases Suggestive of Reincarnation.* 2nd ed. Charlottesville: University Press of Virginia.
Stevenson, Ian. 1980. *Cases of the Reincarnation Type. Volume 3: Twelve Cases in Lebanon and Turkey*. Charlottesville: University Press of Virginia.
Stevenson, Ian. 1984. Unlearned Language: New Studies in Xenoglossy. Charlottesville: University Press of Virginia.
Stevenson, Ian. 2001. *Children Who Remember Previous Lives*. Jefferson, NC: McFarland.
Swinburne, Richard. 1984. "Personal Identity: The Dualist Theory." In Personal Identity, edited by Sydney Shoemaker and Richard Swinburne, 1–66. Oxford: Blackwell.
Thomason, Sarah. 1988. Reply to "Response to 'Past Tongues Remembered?'" Skeptical Inquirer 12, no. 3 (Spring): 323–24. https://skepticalinquirer.org/wp-content/uploads/sites/29/2019/03/Issue-03-9.pdf.
Thomason, Sarah. 1987. "Past Tongues Remembered?" Skeptical Inquirer 11, no. 4 (Summer): 367–75. https://skepticalinquirer.org/1987/07/past-tongues-remembered/.
Tucker, Jim B. 2013. Return to Life: Extraordinary Cases of Children who Remember Past Lives. New York: St. Martin's Griffin.
Wheatley, James M. O. 1995. Review of *Death and Personal Survival: The Evidence of Life After Death*, by Robert Almeder. Journal of Scientific Exploration 9, no. 2 (June): 294.

Williams, B. O. A. 1956-1957. "Personal Identity and Individuation." Proceedings of the Aristotelian Society n.s. 57, 229–53. Oxford: Oxford University Press. https://www.jstor.org/stable/4544578.

Additional Suggested Reading

Almeder, Robert 1987. *Beyond Death: Evidence for Life After Death.* Springfield, IL: Charles C. Thomas.

Almeder, Robert. 1990. Review of *Children Who Remember Previous Lives*, by Ian Stevenson. *Journal of the American Society for Psychical Research* 84, no. 1 (January).

Almeder, Robert. 2012. "The Major Objections from Reductive Materialism Against Cartesian Mind-Body Dualism." In *Exploring Frontiers of the Mind-Brain Relationship*, edited by Alexander Moreira-Almeida and Franklin Santana Santos, 17-33. New York: Springer. [This is a shortened and revised version translated with my permission into Portuguese and published in *Psiquiatria Clinica* 4 (2013): 150–57.]

Blackburn, Simon. 1994. *The Oxford Dictionary of Philosophy*. Oxford: Oxford University Press. s.v. "Consciousness."

Block, Ned. 1993. Review of *Consciousness Explained*, by Daniel C. Dennett. *Journal of Philosophy*, 90, no. 4 (April): 181–93. https://doi.org/10.2307/2940970.

Block, Ned, and Jerry A. Fodor. 1972. "What Psychological States Are Not." *Philosophical Review* 81, no. 2 (April): 159–81. https://doi.org/10.2307/2183991.

Braude, Stephen E. 2005. *Immortal Remains: The Evidence of Life After Death*. Lanham, MD: Rowman & Littlefield.

Chalmers, David J. 1995. "The Puzzle of Conscious Experience." *Scientific American* 273, no. 6 (December): 80–86. https://doi.org/10.1038/scientificamerican1295-80.

Chalmers, David J. 2002. *Philosophy of Mind: Classical and Contemporary Readings.* Oxford: Oxford University Press.

Dennett, Daniel C. 1982. "How to Study Consciousness Empirically; or Nothing Comes to Mind." *Syntheses* 53, no. 2 (November): 159–80. http://hdl.handle.net/10427/56702.

Dennett, Daniel C. 2005. *Sweet Dreams: Philosophical Obstacles to a Science of Consciousness.* Cambridge, MA: MIT Press.

Eccles, John C. 1994. *How the Self Controls Its Brain*. Berlin: Springer-Verlag.

Fodor, Jerry A. 1998. *In Critical Condition: Polemical Essays on Cognitive Science and the Philosophy of Mind*. Cambridge, MA: MIT Press.

Goldman, Alvin I. 1997. "Science, Publicity, and Consciousness." *Philosophy of Science* 64, no. 4 (December): 525–45. https://www.jstor.org/stable/188559.

Goldman, Alvin I. 2000. "Can Science Know When You Are Conscious?" *Journal of Consciousness Studies* 7, no. 5 (May): 3–22.

Greco, John. 2000. *Putting Skeptics In Their Place: The Nature of Skeptical Arguments and their Role in Philosophical Inquiry*. Cambridge: Cambridge University Press.

Grossman, Neal. 2014. *Healing the Mind: The Philosophy of Spinoza Adapted For a New Age*. Cranberry, NJ: Susquehanna Press.

Grossman, Neal. 2019. *Conversations with Socrates and Plato: How A Post-Materialist Social Order Can Solve the Challenges of Modern Life and Insure Our Survival*. Alresford, UK: Iff Books.

Hawthorne, John. 2004. "Why Humans Are Out of Their Minds." *Noûs* 38, no. 2 (June): 351–58. https://doi.org/10.1111/j.1468-0068.2004.00473.x.

Heil, John, and Alfred Mele, eds. 1993. *Mental Causation*. New York: Oxford University Press.

Hempel, Carl G. 1965. *Aspects of Scientific Explanation and Other Essays in the Philosophy of Science*. New York: Free Press.

Hill, Christopher S. 1997. "Imaginability, Conceivability, Possibility and the Mind-Body Problem." *Philosophical Studies* 87, no. 1 (July): 61–85. https://doi.org/10.1023/A:1017911200883.

Hill, Christopher S. 2009. *Consciousness*. Cambridge: Cambridge University Press.

Hofstadter, Douglas R., and Daniel C. Dennett, eds. 1981. *The Mind's I: Fantasies and Reflections on Self and Soul*. New York: Basic Books.

Humphrey, Nicholas. 2000. "How to Solve the Mind-Body Problem." *Journal of Consciousness Studies* 7, no. 4 (January): 5–20. https://philpapers.org/rec/HUMHTS.

Humphreys, Paul. 1997. "How Properties Emerge." *Philosophy of Science* 64, no. 1 (March): 1–17. https://www.jstor.org/stable/188367.

Jackson, Frank. 1982. "Epiphenomenal Qualia." *Philosophical Quarterly* 32, no. 127 (April): 127–36. https://doi.org/10.2307/2960077.

James, William. 1898/1956. "Human Immortality: Two Supposed Objections to the Doctrine." In *William James on Psychical Research*, compiled and edited by Gardner Murphy & Robert O. Ballou, 279–308. New York: Viking Press.

Kind, Amy 2005. "The Irreducibility of Consciousness." *Disputatio* 1, no. 19 (November): 237–47. https://doi.org/10.2478/disp-2005-0010.

Levine, Joseph. 1983. "Materialism and Qualia: The Explanatory Gap." *Pacific Philosophical Quarterly* 64, no. 4 (October): 354–61. https://doi.org/10.1111/j.1468-0114.1983.tb00207.x.

Levine, Joseph. 1994. "Out of the Closet: A Qualophile Confronts Qualophobia." *Philosophical Topics* 22, nos. 1/2 (Spring and Fall): 107–26. https://www.jstor.org/stable/43154655.

Lewis, David. 1966. "An Argument for the Identity Theory." *Journal of Philosophy* 63, no. 1 (January): 17–25. https://doi.org/10.2307/2024524.

Lewis, David. 2001a. "Counterparts or Double Lives?" In *Metaphysics: Contemporary Readings*, edited by Michael J. Loux, 188–217. London: Routledge

Lewis, David. 2001b. "Survival and Identity." In *Metaphysics: Contemporary Readings*, edited by Michael J. Loux, 395–411. London: Routledge.

Lycan, William G. 1987. *Consciousness*. Cambridge, MA: MIT Press.

Lycan, William G. 1996. *Consciousness and Experience*. Cambridge, MA: MIT Press.

Lycan, William G. 2008. "Phenomenal Intentionalities." *American Philosophical Quarterly* 45, no. 3 (July): 233–52. https://www.jstor.org/stable/20464415

Lycan, William G. 2013. "Is Property Dualism Better Off Than Substance Dualism?" *Philosophical Studies* 164, no. 2 (June): 533–42. https://www.jstor.org/stable/41932742.

McGinn, Colin. 1989. "Can We Solve the Mind-Body Problem? *Mind* 98, no. 391 (July): 349–66. https://www.jstor.org/stable/2254848.

Nagel, Thomas. 1974. "What Is It Like to Be a Bat?" *Philosophical Review* 83, no. 4 (October): 435–50. https://doi.org/10.2307/2183914.

Nagel, Thomas. 1979. *Mortal Questions*. Cambridge: Cambridge University Press.

Nagel, Thomas. 1998. "Conceiving the Impossible and the Mind-Body Problem." *Philosophy* 73, no. 285 (July): 337–52. https://www.jstor.org/stable/3751987.

Quinton, Anthony. 1962. "The Soul." *Journal of Philosophy* 59, no. 15 (July): 393–409. https://doi.org/10.2307/2022957.

Shoemaker, Sydney. 2007. *Physical Realization*. Oxford: Oxford University Press.

Strawson, Galen. 1992. "The Self as Software." Review of *Consciousness Explained*, by Daniel Dennett. Times Literary Supplement 4664 (August 21): 5–6. https://www.academia.edu/411597/The_self_as_software_1992_review_of_Dennett_Consciousness_Explained.

Swinburne, Richard. 1973-1974. "Personal Identity." *Proceedings of the Aristotelian Society* 74, 3–35. Oxford: Oxford University Press. https://www.jstor.org/stable/i408499.

Tucker, Jim B. 2005. *Life Before Life: A Scientific Investigation of Children's Memories of Previous Lives*. New York: St. Martin's Griffin.

Vision, Gerald. 1998. "Blindsight and Philosophy." *Philosophical Psychology* 11, no. 2: 137–59. https://doi.org/10.1080/09515089808573253.

Vision, Gerald. 2005. "Truly Justified Belief." *Synthese* 146, no. 3 (September): 403–40. http://dx.doi.org/10.1007/s11229-004-6228-0.

Vision, Gerald. 2011. *Re-Emergence: Locating Conscious Properties in a Material World*. Cambridge, MA: MIT Press.

Wheatley, James M. O. [Melville Owen]. 1979. "Reincarnation, 'Astral Bodies' and 'Psi-Components.'" *Journal of the American Society for Psychical Research* 73, no. 2 (April): 109–22.

Woodward, Jim. 2007. "Causation with a Human Face." In *Causation, Physics, and the Constitution of Reality: Russell's Republic Revisited*, edited by Huw Price and Richard Corry, 66–105. Oxford: Oxford University Press.

Zawidzki, Tadeusz Wieslaw. 2007. *Dennett*. Oxford: One World.

Index

agreement among philosophers, lack of, 3–4
Almeder, Robert, 80, 83
appeal to the general population (*ad populum*), 15
"Are 'Past Life' Regressions Evidence of Reincarnation?" (Harris), 50–51
Aristotle, 4
arm, raising of, 18–19
Arther, Richard, 38
Ayer, A. J., 7, 9, 10–11, 26, 27; on bodily continuity, 97, 99n1; on Caesar experiment, 10, 63n1, 85–86, 99n1; on Cartesian Immaterial Substances, 99n1; "The Concept of a Person" by, 97–98, 99n1; on memory theory of personal identity, 99n1; on Parfit, 69; Wheatley on, 85

Banerjee, H. N., 41
Bengali, 42
biological feature, consciousness as, 11–13, 16, 19–20, 91–92, 93–94; scientific evidence for, 14–15
biological product, memory as, 9
Blackmore, Susan, 87
bodiless person, as incoherent, 81–83, 98

bodily continuity, 57–58, 63, 81–82, 84; Ayer on, 97, 99n1
brain, as carrier of memories, 6
Braude, Stephen E., 73–76, 78–79, 88
Broad, C. D., 18, 82–83
Brown, John, 36

Caesar, Julius, 7–8, 9, 22–24, 26, 55; Ayer on experiment with, 10, 63n1, 85–86, 99n1
Caesar on park bench experiment, 22–24, 26–27, 59, 61–62, 84–86; Ayer on, 10, 63n1, 85–86, 99n1
"Can a Man Witness His Own Funeral?" (Flew), 69
Carnap, Rudolph, 77
carrier of memories, brain as, 6
Cartesian Ego, 5–7, 25
Cartesian Immaterial Substances, 1; Ayer on, 99n1; consciousness as, 95; as explanation of human behavior, 17–20, 83; objections to, 3–5, 89–90; reincarnation and, 21, 72, 90–92; testability of, 4, 7–11, 89
Cartesian Material Substances, 1–2
Cartesian minds, need, for, 15–16
Cathars (dissident group), 33–35
The Cathars and Reincarnation (Guirdham), 33–35

causal agent, without physical body, 84
causality, 17
causation, mental, 91–92
Celtic warrior, Japanese woman and, 5–6, 25–26, 68
changing nature, of scientific discoveries, 4, 84
Charles (in experiment of Reid), 8–9, 64n2
Chhatarpur, India, 41–42
Children Who Remember Past Lives (Stevenson), 54
Cleopatra, 71
closer examination, of paranormal claims, 87–88
"The Concept of a Person" (Ayer), 97–98, 99n1
The Concept of a Person and Other Essays (Ayer), 85
conditions, of Parfit, 26–27
consciousness: as Cartesian Immaterial Substance, 95; existence of, 93–94; as neurobiological state, 9, 11, 13, 16, 19
consciousness, as biological feature, 11–13, 16, 19–20, 91–92, 93–94; scientific evidence for, 14–15
Consciousness Explained (Dennett), 20n2
continuity: bodily, 57–58, 63, 81–82, 84, 97, 99n1; psychological, 6–7
core features, of Stevenson, 28–29, 49–50, 51–52
Corsair airplane, 45–46
Cratylus Maximus (from Caesar experiment), 7, 23
cryptomnesia, 29, 50–51, 64n3

Davis, Dorothy, 38
Death and Personal Survival (Almeder), 68, 75, 79–87
deductive implications, at sensory level, 77
Dennett, Daniel, 20n2, 93–94
Descartes, René, 3, 21, 73, 79

dinosaurs, reincarnation compared with, 55–56, 69–70
Division of Parapsychology at University of Virginia Medical School, 92
Duvernoy (Professor), 35

Eberswalde, Germany, 39–40
Eisenbud, Jule, 73
empirical testing: pragmatic considerations in, 77–78; of reincarnation hypothesis, 22–27, 55–56, 57–59, 69–70, 95
epistemic sense, of irrationality, 80–81
epistemology, naturalized, 14
Erika Gottlieb (in Stevenson), 39
ESP, 73, 75
Essays on the Intellectual Powers of Man (Reid), 8, 64n2
essential elements, of person, 22, 61, 91
"Evaluating the Super-Psi Hypothesis" (Braude), 76
"Evidenfalsifiability, of hypothesis, 77ce and the Afterlife" (Hales), 70
evil demon hypothesis, 73
existence: of consciousness, 93–94; of dinosaurs reincarnation compared with, 55–56, 69–70; of souls, 4
explanation of human behavior, Cartesian Immaterial Substances as, 17–20, 83

factual incoherence, logical incoherence contrasted with, 82
falsifiability, of hypothesis, 77
family, leading questions of, 53–54
Fawkes, Guy, 8–9, 64n2
Flew, Antony, 69
Fodor, Jerry, 94
Franklin, Christine Ladd, 4
fraud, in paranormal claims, 87–88
Frau Schilder (in Stevenson), 39

genetic memory, 51–52
Goodall, Jane, 4

Gretchen Gottlieb (in Stevenson), 37–40, 50, 51, 53, 64n4
Guirdham, Arthur, 33–35

Hales, Steven, 67, 69, 72; on Parfit, 68, 71
Harris, Melvin, 50–51
Hempel, Carl G., 76
Herman Gottlieb (in Stevenson), 39
higher level pragmatic considerations, 77
History of Harrison County, West Virginia (Davis), 38
"How a Non-Reductionist View Might Have Been True" (Parfit), 5–7
human behavior, 83; mechanistic explanations of, 19–20; science and, 18
Huston, James, 44–48
hypnotism, 36

ideal case, of Stevenson, 29–30, 64nn3–4
identity, of reincarnated person, 59–61
immaterial minds, 91–92
Immortal Remains (Braude), 73
incoherent, bodiless person, as, 81–83, 98
In Critical Condition (Fodor), 94
insanity, irrationality contrasted with, 80
irrationality: epistemic sense of, 80–81
Iwo Jima, 44–48

Japanese woman, Celtic warrior and, 5–6, 25–26, 68
Jay, Carroll, 37–39
Jay, Dolores, 37–39, 50, 53
Jensen Jacoby (in Stevenson), 36–37, 50, 51, 53
Johnson, Harold, 36
Johnson, Lydia, 36, 50, 51–52, 53
Journal of Scientific Exploration (journal), 67

Kapoor, Bishen Chand, 30–33, 51, 55, 59–60, 73
Kapoor, Kamla, 31
Katni, India, 41
Kim, Jaegwon, 91–92, 94
kinetic energy: for physical objects only, 18, 82, 96; transfer, of, 17–19, 82
knowledge, private, 78

Lang d'Oc language, 33
Larsen, Jack, 43, 45–47
Latvia (in Stevenson), 37
Lazarus Smart (in data of Stevenson), 28
leading questions, of family, 53–54
Lectures on Physical Research (Broad), 18, 82–83
Leininger, Andrea, 44–45, 47, 49, 64n6
Leininger, Bruce, 44–48, 64n6
Leininger, James, 43–47, 64n6, 92, 95
Levine, Joseph, 19–20
The Limits of Influence (Braude), 75
linguistic objection, to reincarnation, 52–53
logical incoherence, factual incoherence contrasted with, 82

materialism: neo-classical, 15; reductive, 1–2, 16, 17, 70, 72, 89–90, 93
mechanistic explanations, of human behavior, 19–20
memories: of reincarnated person, 10, 60–61, 71, 90–91, 95, 98, 99n1; verification of, 23–24, 62, 71
memory: as biological product, 9; genetic, 51–52; physical body and, 58, 63, 86
memory acquisition, reincarnation contrasted with, 85–86, 97–98, 99n1
memory theory of personal identity, 8–11, 23–26, 62, 65n8, 76, 96, 99n1
mental and material, as mutually exclusive, 15, 90
mental causation, 91–92

mental events, physical objects and, 90, 94, 96
methodological objection, to reincarnation, 54–55, 64n7, 86–88
"Mind-Body Identity, Privacy, and Categories" (Rorty), 15
mind-body problem, 1–2, 12, 95
minds: immaterial, 91–92; non-physical, 1
Minimalist Reincarnation Hypothesis, 21, 71, 90–91; testability of, 22–27, 55–56, 57–59, 69–70, 95
Mishra, Sri M. L., 41, 43
Mishra, Swarnlata, 41–43
mutually exclusive, mental and material, as, 15, 90

Narain, Laxmi, 31–33, 51, 59–60, 73
Natoma (ship), 44, 46–48
naturalized epistemology, 14
Nelli, René, 33, 35
neo-classical materialism, 15
neurobiological state, consciousness, as, 9, 11, 13, 16, 19
non-physical minds, 1

OBE. *See* Out-of-Body Experience
objections, to Cartesian Immaterial Substances, 3–5, 89–90
occurrence, of reincarnation, 83–84, 91, 96
one person, reincarnated person as, 98
Out-of-Body Experience (OBE), 87

Padma (in Stevenson), 31–32
Pandy family, 41–43
Paramnesia, 53–54
paranormal claims: closer examination of, 87–88; fraud in, 87–88
paranormal knowledge (PK), 42, 73–75, 79
Parfit, Derek, 5–6, 9, 11, 25; Ayer on, 69; conditions of, 26–27; on confirmable nature of reincarnation, 89; Hales on, 68, 71; on reincarnation memories and, 86
past lives, 31–53, 92–93, 95; potential for error in cases of, 54–55; skills from, 28–30, 32, 33–40, 62
"Past Tongues Remembered?" (Thomason), 52–53
Pathak, Biya, 41–43
Pathak family, 41–43
Penelhum, Terrence, 57–58, 62–63, 80, 81–82
Penelhum Objection, 57–59, 62–63
person, essential elements of, 22, 61, 91
personal: reincarnation theory of, 2, 5–11, 23–26, 67; survival post-mortem, 79–82, 87–88
personal identity, memory theory of, 8–11, 23–26, 62, 65n8, 76, 96; Ayer on, 99n1
Philosophia (Journal), 67
philosophical scandal (*scandalum philosophiae*), 3
philosophical solipsism, 3–4
philosophy, religion and, 1, 3, 12, 13
Philosophy of Natural Science (Hempel), 76
physical body: causal agent without, 84; memories and, 58, 63, 86
physicalism, 22, 89, 91, 95–96
Physicalism, or Something Near Enough (Kim), 91–92
physicalists, 22, 89
physical objects: kinetic energy only for, 18, 82, 96; mental events and, 90, 94, 96
Pilibhit, India, 30–31
PK. *See* paranormal knowledge
population objection, to reincarnation, 56–57
possibility, of fraud in reincarnation cases, 87
post-mortem personal survival, 79–82, 87–88
potential, for error in past life cases, 54–55

pragmatic considerations, in empirical testing, 77–78
pragmatic considerations, in testing of hypothesis, 77–78
Principle of Conservation of Energy, 17, 82
Principle of Parsimony, 15–16
private knowledge, 78
problem, mind-body, 1–2, 12, 95
The Problem of Knowledge (Ayer), 7, 10, 26, 63n1, 85–86, 99n1
Psi, 73–79, 88
Psi-Hypothesis, 73–79, 88
psychological continuity, 6–7
Purple Haze (Levine), 19–20

qualia, 94–95
Quintus (from Caesar experiment), 23

raising, of arm, 18–19
Reasons and Persons (Parfit), 5–7, 25–26
The Rediscovery of Mind (Searle), 11–12
reductive materialism, 1–2, 16, 17, 70, 72; arguments of, 89–90, 93
Reid, Thomas, 8, 64n2
reincarnated person: identity of, 59–61; memories of, 10, 60–61, 71, 90–91, 95, 98, 99n1; as one person, 98
reincarnation: acquisition of memories contrasted with, 85–86, 97–98, 99n1; Cartesian Immaterial Substances and, 21, 72, 90–92; existence of dinosaurs compared with, 55–56, 69–70; linguistic objection to, 52–53; occurrence of, 83–84, 91, 96; Penelhum objection to, 57–59, 62–63; population objection to, 56–57; possibility of fraud in cases of, 87
"Reincarnation and the Practice of Medicine" (Guirdham), 35
reincarnation hypothesis, 21; linguistic objection to, 52–53; methodological objection to, 54–55, 64n7, 86–88; Penelhum objection to, 57–58; population objection to, 56–57
"Reincarnation Redux" (Hales), 70
religion, philosophy and, 1, 3, 12, 13
Return to Life (Tucker), 44
"Review of *Death and Personal Survival*" (Wheatley), 80, 83–85
Robert (in experiment of Williams), 8–9, 64n2
Roger de Grisolles (in Guirdham), 33–34
Rorty, Richard, 15
Russell, Bertrand, 4, 80

Sahay, K. K. N., 31, 32
Sander Lal (in Stevenson), 32
schizophrenia, 84
science: human behavior and, 18; theoretical elements of, 56, 84
scientific discoveries, changing nature of, 4, 84
scientific evidence, for biological nature of consciousness, 14–15
scientific worldview, 14, 92–93
Searle, John R., 5, 11–15, 16, 89
sensory level, deductive implications at, 77
skills, from past life, 28–30, 32, 33–40, 62
Smith (Mr.), 57–58, 80
Smith (Mrs.), 33–35, 50
sneaky Psi, 75, 76, 78
solipsism, philosophical, 3–4
souls, 4
Stevenson, Ian, 27, 53, 72, 85, 92; *Children Who Remember Past Lives* by, 54; core features of, 28–29, 49–50, 51–52; Gretchen case and, 37–40; ideal case of, 29–30, 64nn3–4; Swarlata case and, 41–42; *Twenty Cases Suggestive of Reincarnation* by, 27–28; *Unlearned Language* by, 36, 38–40; *Xenoglossy* by, 36
Super Psi, 73–79

Supervenience, 94
Survival and Disembodied Existence (Penelhum), 57–58, 62–63
survival evidence, 74
"Survival or Super-Psi?" (Braude), 74
Swarlata case, Stevenson and, 41–42
Sweet Dreams (Dennett), 93–94

testability: of Cartesian Immaterial Substances, 4, 7–11, 89; of existence of souls, 4, 7–10; of minimalist reincarnation hypothesis, 22–27, 55–56, 57–59, 69–70, 95; of Psi and Super-Psi, 75–79
theoretical elements, of science, 56, 84
Thomason, Sarah, 52–53
transfer, of kinetic energy, 17–19, 82
Tucker, James "Jim" B., 44–46, 48, 64n6
Twenty Cases Suggestive of Reincarnation (Stevenson), 27–28

Unlearned Language (Stevenson), 36, 38–40
Urdu language, 32

verification, of memories, 23–24, 62, 71
Virgilius (from Caesar experiment), 23–24

Washington, George, 98
Wheatley, James M. O., 79–84; on Ayer, 85
Williams, B.O.A, 8–9, 64n2
worldview, scientific, 14, 92–93
Wright, Robert, 93

Xenoglossy, 36–38, 50, 51–52, 54, 73–74
Xenoglossy (Stevenson), 36

About the Author

Robert Almeder, PhD, received his doctorate in Philosophy from the University of Pennsylvania. Under a National Science Foundation (NSF) grant he did post-doctoral work in the Philosophy of Science at Stanford University. As a past Fulbright Senior Research Fellow, teaching at both Tel Aviv University (1992) and later at the National Research Center in Paris (1992 and 1994), he lectured occasionally in Philosophy of Science and Epistemology at the Sorbonne and elsewhere in France and Europe. He was also a Senior Research Fellow at the Center for the History and Philosophy of Science at the University of Pittsburgh (1984 and 1988) and was a Senior Research Associate in the Ecole Polytechnique (CREA) at the National Research Center in Paris during the fall semester of 1996, and in 2004. As a current Fulbright Senior Specialist in American Studies, specializing in Philosophy of Science and Epistemology, he taught American Philosophy at the National University in Berkina Faso (Africa) in 2007. He served as the Chairman of the Fulbright Commission Panel for the discipline of Philosophy (1993–1995) and also served (2005–2006) as the Inaugural McCullough Distinguished Visiting Professor in Ethics and Political Philosophy at Hamilton College, New York. For five years he served as the Editor of *The American Philosophical Quarterly* and spent most of his time teaching and writing in the department of Philosophy at Georgia State University where he was a Distinguished University Professor. He has been a research proposal referee and consultant to the NSF, and also a frequent research panelist for the National Endowment for Humanities and an ethical consultant for the U.S. Centers for Disease Control and Prevention and the U.S. Department of Justice, medical institutions, and law firms.

He has published over one hundred peer-reviewed essays in various premiere philosophy journals. Several of his essays in *Theory of Knowledge*, *Philosophy of Science*, and *Journal of Business Ethics* re-appear in other collections. He has published (copublished or coedited) several (twenty-six) books and has others pending publication.

Among his published books are *The Philosophy of Charles S. Peirce: A Critical Introduction* (Basil Blackwell, 1980); *Blind Realism: An Essay on*

Human Knowledge and Natural Science (Rowman & Littlefield, 1992); *Death and Personal Survival: The Evidence for Life After Death* (Rowman & Littlefield, 1992); *Harmless Naturalism: The Limits of Science and the Nature of Philosophy* (Open Court, 1998); *Human Happiness and Morality: A Brief Introduction to Ethics* (Prometheus, 2000); *Truth and Skepticism* (Rowman & Littlefield, 2010); and *Global Warming: The Skeptic's Brief* (Stairway Press, 2015).

He has served on the Board of Editors for *The American Philosophical Quarterly, Public Affairs Quarterly, The History of Philosophy Quarterly, The Journal of Business Ethics, Philosophy Research Archives, The Journal of Value Inquiry, Philosophia,* and *The Transactions of the Charles S. Peirce Society.*

www.ingramcontent.com/pod-product-compliance
Lightning Source LLC
Chambersburg PA
CBHW052052220426
43663CB00012B/2544